BASIC UNDERSTAN

UK FINANCIAL *System*

...PRACTICAL GUIDE TO BUILDING PERSONAL WEALTH PORTFOLIO

Dear Alison,
Nice meeting you
at the Networking
event and looking
forward to hearing from
you again
Best wishes!

NIYI MURELE

BASIC UNDERSTANDING OF UK FINANCIAL SYSTEM
Guide to Building Personal Wealth Portfolio

by
Niyi Murele

Published by:
AyanfeOluwa Publishing Services
+234 708 9203 076
info@coachayanfeoluwa.com

ISBN
979-882-464-134-9

CONTENTS

ACKNOWLEDGMENT

This book has taken more time than envisaged to become a reality. However, all thanks and glory to God for giving me the gift of life and wisdom to make the book possible.

The encouragement of my darling wife Olusade is highly commendable. Thank you Sweetheart!

Sincere appreciation to Mrs. Kemi Shoyoye for proof-reading and editing the manuscript. You are highly appreciated.

And to Oluwaseun Ayanfeoluwa, thanks for all your hard work towards publishing the book.

PREFACE

I was not born in Britain. I was born and raised in Nigeria. I later migrated to Britain when l got married to my beautiful wife who happens to be a British citizen.

In all my years of living in Nigeria, l cannot remember a single occasion where someone spoke to me about financial literacy or wealth creation. Interestingly, within my family and circle of friends, we all desired to be wealthy in life, but we had no clue how to create wealth, neither were we financially literate. The best we were told was to go to school, get a job after and earn an income for survival. Throughout my years in school, l cannot remember taking any course on wealth creation or entrepreneurship.

However, l was privileged to live with my mum (of blessed memory), who was a trader and sold various products such as beer, cement, groundnut oil, kolanuts, snacks. etc. I was involved in her business activities including hawking some of the products. In the process, l made some stipends, but wasn't conscious of the entrepreneurial aspect of what l was doing.

After my first degree, l began to search for a job, and unfortunately that became an uphill task. I eventually got a temporary teaching role at the Federal Government College, Kwali, Abuja in Nigeria. Thc employment however only lasted five months because I was required to regularise my teaching appointment at the Federal Ministry of Education in Lagos State, Nigeria. After going to the Ministry of Education's office severally without any success, I gave up. I stayed back in Lagos and that was where I began to have exposure to the business world. I lived with a supposed businessman whose operations were within his flat. It was there that all business transactions and client meetings were discussed in an atmosphere of pleasure. As an errand boy in that environment, I made more money than what I was earning as a teacher and began to learn about the business, including the process of business incorporation, imports and exports procedure. I also acquired some basic business management skills. To some extent, even though I had no regular income, I became financially better than many of my graduate friends who were employed and earning salaries. This was the beginning of my journey into the business world. With that mini business experience, I figured out the reason why there is always a wide financial gap between earning an income and running a business.

The real change came when I joined my wife in the United Kingdom and found myself in a different environment. Shortly after my arrival, my wife proposed that we buy our own property. I nearly fainted because my mind could not comprehend how on earth to achieve that. Remember I just came from an environment and background where only the rich owned properties which they built from the scratch with loans from mortgage banks.

My wife works in a bank and knew better. She began to educate me on what it takes to buy a property in the United Kingdom, the types of government schemes and mortgage provisions available to help individuals acquire properties instead of renting. The education helped a lot, but she still met a wall of resistance from me until I experienced a breakthrough in my mind. After that, l asked her to let us commence the property purchase process. We went to see a mortgage broker who gave us an idea of the maximum amount of mortgage borrowing we could get from the lender based on our household income. From that meeting, we realised we may need to take advantage of "Shared Ownership Scheme" as we didn't have enough income to shoulder required mortgage for the average property price in our chosen location. I wasn't particularly excited about the shared ownership scheme, but I realised that being partly landlord and partly tenant is better than being hundred percent tenant! In addition, I figured out that we will have a new house that is bigger and better than our studio flat. We also had the option of increasing our stake in the property as and when we have the resources to do so. The more understanding l had, the better decisions l made.

We bought our first property with just 40% equity contribution and ownership. We moved from a studio flat to a three-bedroom house in an upcoming area. After five years, we bought out the remaining Housing Association equity of 60% by which time the property had gone up in value to £163,000.00 from the original purchase price of £92,000.00. In five years, the property had appreciated by £71,000.00!

Of course, only forty percent of that was ours while the remaining sixty percent belonged to the housing association. But we were £28,400.00 richer, by part ownership from our share of the equity on the property, which formed part of the funds we used in buying out the Housing Association after five years.

Not only did l learn so much about the dynamics of the shared ownership scheme, I also discovered that you could make money from owning your own property and by using other people's money. However, the real 'biggie' for me at that time was that, gradually I began to understand the system. I experienced the possibility of creating wealth by acquiring knowledge and understanding the system.

Today, we have been able to create a portfolio of investment properties just from that first purchase via shared ownership scheme.

As I write this book several years after the experience narrated above, there are still thousands of people out there who have been tenants in the system for a very long time, with absolutely no clue about the opportunities that exist within the system. They work and earn an income, but are not able to create wealth despite all the available legitimate avenues to do so.

Working and earning an income on its own does not automatically translate into wealth creation. You must know what to do with your earnings to create wealth. It is for this reason that I have taken the pains of writing this book. My almost two decades of experience in Great Britain's financial services industry re-confirms that without basic understanding of the financial system of a nation, you cannot make much of the opportunities that exist within the system. Now by hindsight, l can see the reason why many remain poor despite their earnings and degrees amid opportunities that exist around them.

Basic understanding of the financial system of a nation can turn the fortunes of many around like it did for me.

This book will not only enlighten, but also bring about a shift in your understanding of Britain's financial system, as well as equip you to make smart financial decisions about the many opportunities that surround you.

Finally, let me add that although the contents of this book zeroed in on Britain's financial system, the core principles of wealth creation and strategies are universal and can be applied globally in different nations. All it takes is understanding and application of the principles.

Best wishes...

INTRODUCTION

When you gain understanding in any subject, it results in acquisition of knowledge. Knowledge is powerful. The difference between an average individual and the many millionaires that you and I know is that the millionaires know something that others don't know, and through that knowledge they have acquired their millions. Your position will never change if all you knew last year is the same as you do this year. In order to change any aspect of your life, you must search for relevant knowledge in that area. It is an established fact that the more you know, the more value you add to your life, and ultimately, your position will change. The world today is in search of knowledge, and only those who have it are in a position to provide solutions to problems while others are eager to pay for these solutions. This fact is the bedrock of many successful entrepreneurs. They deploy the knowledge they have in providing solutions to people's problems and get paid for doing so.

Robert Kiyosaki, a Real Estate guru in his bestselling book,*'Rich Dad, Poor Dad'* painted vivid pictures of his two dads for us to see the difference between them. In summary, the rich dad knew something that the poor dad didn't know, and what the poor dad knew was not enough to change his financial position. Warren Buffet is the fourth wealthiest man in the world and second wealthiest in America. In the world of investment, he is referred to as a *'wizard'* because he knew what other investors did not know. When Bill Gates dropped out of the university to follow his instinct on technology and personal computers, it was because he knew something that many in the corporate world at that time didn't know. Through this knowledge, he has impacted the world tremendously, becoming a household name and global icon. We can continue to document successful men dominating our world today, and the discovery will still be the same- that they did so through the power of knowledge. I have taken time to lay this foundation because of its significance in our subject of discussion– 'The Financial System' in the United Kingdom.

...the rich dad knew something that the poor dad didn't know, and what the poor dad knew was not enough to change his financial position.

Webster dictionary defines 'System' as follows:

(I) *a regularly interacting or interdependent group of items forming a unified whole, an organised set of doctrines, ideas, or principles usually intended to explain the arrangement of working of a systematic whole,*

(ii) *An organised or established procedure, harmonious arrangement or pattern, and lastly (iii) an organised society or social situation regarded as stultifying or oppressive.*

From the definitions above, there are suggestions that a system is made of many inter-twined concepts working together to the benefits of those who understand it. Without proper understanding of a particular system, you cannot profit from it. This is the case with the financial system of United Kingdom. Although full of opportunities and potentials for wealth building, only people who are knowledgeable about and understand it can profit from it. In addition, it is established, institutionalised and complex, as the government continues to add layers annually through introduction of new policies deemed to be financially beneficial to the general populace. To benefit from it therefore, you must be abreast of continual changes implemented by the government in various areas of the financial system and industries.

The financial services industry is the major strength of UK's economy. Without a proper understanding of how it works, it may be difficult, if not impossible, to interpret its dynamics effectively.

One of the major objectives of this book is to help readers to connect the system with the economy and make informed decisions about government policies pertaining to the industry. What I have put together here is both simple and straightforward, yet sufficient in assisting interested readers to find their feet and take appropriate actions in achieving their financial objectives.

SECTION ONE

UNITED KINGDOM: THE FINANCIAL SYSTEM AND ECONOMY

UNITED KINGDOM: THE FINANCIAL SYSTEM AND ECONOMY

According to a briefing paper presented to the House of Commons by Gloria Tyler dated 31st of March, 2017 (Briefing Paper 6193):

In 2016, financial and insurance services contributed £124.2 billion in gross value added (GVA) to the UK economy, 7.2% of the UK's total GVA. London accounted for 51% of the total financial and insurance sector GVA in the UK in 2015. There are over one million jobs in the financial and insurance sector (3.1% of all UK jobs). The UK had a surplus of over £60 billion on trade in the financial and insurance sectors in 2016. In 2015-16, the banking sector alone contributed £24.4 billion to UK tax receipts in corporation tax, income tax, national insurance and through the bank levy. (Briefing Paper 6193)

From the briefing paper, the industry impacts on three major areas of the economy – Gross Value Added (GVA), jobs and corporation tax. As a result, the government is extremely proactive where the financial services industry is concerned. Whatever affects the sector will impact significantly on the economy. To ensure continuity of growth year in year out, any government of the day knows that the industry is first among equals for notable attention. Positive measures are put in place consistently to attract investors within and outside the country and to also boost their confidence. Such measures encourage stakeholder firms to be creative in developing products that attracts investors globally.

Gloria Tyler in her paper confirmed that the United Kingdom recorded a trade surplus of £43.8 billion. This simply means the country exported more services in the financial sector in excess of £43.8 billion in comparison with financial services transactions imported into the country. This indicates that there are opportunities within the sector that investors are looking for and are equally ready to pay for in order to add value to their financial plans and objectives.

Unfortunately, many individuals who live in the UK may not be aware of these opportunities because they have not made conscious efforts to research the system and how it operates. In my interactions with different people, I discovered that they have the resources to improve and strengthen their financial position, but lack the knowledge of what to do. This is my main motivation for writing the book you are reading. I have met many people who strongly desired to invest in the stock markets, real estates, commodities and so on, but pulled back because they don't know how to go about it. Some others made blind efforts and got their fingers burnt in the process. There are however others who understood the system, were able to interpret government measures and policies correctly and are consistently investing in the economy because of the reward they enjoy continually.

FTSE 100 for instance, is made up of top hundred companies in relations to their market capitalisation. The overall market capitalisation of the exchange as at the beginning of 2018 is over £2 trillion. Most companies in this group have global representations in terms of their products and services and some have been inexistence for centuries and decades. Their stocks and shares are therefore traded by many investors, both retail and corporate, within and outside of UK, thereby attracting huge amount of daily inflow and outflow of money into UK economic system. The FTSE 100 fluctuates between 75-80% of total market capital of London Stock Exchange. Other index on are FTSE 250, FTSE 350, FTSE All Share, etc.

Listed companies are made up of representatives of companies from all sectors of the economy. This is what makes financial services to be the rallying point of the economy. It provides a platform of opportunity for investors to invest in different sectors of their choice. The trading of shares of listed companies triggers economic activities as it results in inflow of funds into the economy. Companies can grow their size. To do that, they will have to increase their workforce thereby creating jobs. Manufacturing companies will need to increase their purchase from suppliers. Suppliers will also benefit as their turnover revenues goes up and the chain continues till household income and buying power is better than what it used to be.

I have met many people who strongly desired to invest in the stock markets, real estates, commodities and so on, but pulled back because they don't know how to go about it. Some others made blind efforts and got their fingers burnt in the process.

Inflow of investors' funds also creates huge amount of money in the hand of fund managers who must find ways of growing and multiplying it. Such funds are made available to borrowers of different shapes and sizes with interest charged on it on short, medium and long-term basis. Firms can grow their businesses when capital is available. New companies can start up and SMEs can raise capital to grow their businesses. Availability of funds makes borrowing possible and cheap. All these inter-related activities play a prominent role in the economy of the nation.

Most of the transactions I have mentioned so far have tax implications. Government is able to raise revenues through diverse taxes attributed to different transactions as a result of buying or selling of services. In other sectors, companies with increase in productivity and profit will also pay more corporation tax, while new employees will pay tax and national insurance via the PAYE system. With increased revenues, government can invest more in infrastructure, welfare, health, housing, social security and the list continues.

With such a system in operation, little wonder the government pays attention to activities within the sector.

From the above description, the roles of the financial services industry within the larger economy in the United Kingdom can be summarised into four:

*The industry is a platform through which savings of individuals and corporate organisation are protected, deployed and turned into capital management instruments.

*It brings savers who desire the flexibility of access to their money and borrowers with needs to borrow on longer term for various reasons together through financial firms and institutions, thereby taking longer term position, mediating between both parties and making charges for greater returns.

*Through diverse products of financial instruments, investors are able to spread their risk instead of putting all eggs in one basket. They are able to invest in different assets with different features.

*The industry also helps individuals and companies to protect themselves against possible unforeseen risks which they may not want to expose themselves, but others are willing to, due to their risk appetite.

Chapter Action Points

* Take time to follow economic news and headlines on a daily basis.

* Think of how such news can impact on your personal financial plans.

* Identify an opportunity within the news and how you can access and benefit from them.

2

FINANCIAL STRUCTURE AND STAKEHOLDERS

FINANCIAL STRUCTURE AND STAKEHOLDERS

When the idea of this book occurred to me, I was very clear about its objective. The aim of this book is to provide information that will simplify the workings of United Kingdom's financial system in such away that the average person who reads it will have a measure of confidence to take necessary action about his or her financial position.

It is interesting to know that the system caters for almost everyone who is keen about it. Today in the United Kingdom, you can open an account with just one pound and build up your savings with interests. Although the structure may appear complicated and complex on the outside having been built consistently over decades, in this book, it will be simplified for a better understanding.

The aim of this book is to provide information that will simplify the workings of United Kingdom's financial system in such a way that the average person who reads it will have a measure of confidence to take necessary action about his or her financial position.

The financial structure can be discussed under five main classified headings. These are:

* Financial Infrastructures
* Financial Markets
* Financial Firms and Institutions
* Financial Regulators and Authorities
* The International Stakeholders

Financial Infrastructures

Transactions within the industry are driven by various types of infrastructures which have been put in place such as Trading Systems, Payments Systems, Clearing House and Settlement Systems. The Trading Systems comprise of investment exchanges where daily trading transactions take place and companies can raise capital through initial public offerings on the exchange platform. The Payment Systems are overseen by the Bank of England alongside the money markets. The Clearing House and Settlement Systems provide the platform for the clearance of all securities and derivative instruments. All these infrastructures work together to enhance the operations and smooth flow of the industry. Both wholesale and retail clients employ the infrastructures to manage their financial transactions on a daily basis. Suffice to say that the Payment Council represents the entire banking sector in all matters relating to payments issues.

Financial Markets

The financial markets are made up of the exchange markets and the over-the-counter transactions otherwise referred to as OTC. The exchange is a forum where listed members engage in trading of various forms of investments instruments such as stock and shares of companies otherwise known as equities and derivatives. The process and channels could be electronic or physical exchanges. The London Stock Exchange is a secondary market where securities of bonds and equities are traded after the offer at primary markets via various institutions such as banks. Companies who want to raise capital for the first time do so via primary market as initial public offerings (IPO). Thereafter, stock and shares of such companies are listed on exchange platform, and then traded in the secondary market. The market is regulated by Financial Conduct Authority (FCA). Over-the-Counter markets have no physical exchanges, but stakeholders have an overseer committee who examines their market operations. Apart from London Stock Exchange, other exchange in the United Kingdom includes Alternative Investment Market (AIM) which is a listing platform for small and medium sized firms who are not able to meet the listing parameters of the main stock exchange.

Financial Firms and Institutions

Major financial institutions can be classified under the following agents: -

* Banks and Building Societies
* Life Assurance Companies
* Friendly Societies
* Multi-Products Distributors

-**Banks and Building Societies** – Most banks and Building Societies are the primary outlets of financial services to retail clients. Generally, individuals demonstrate strong loyalties to their banks and building societies from the point of opening an account till death. It is natural for many to make the bank their first point of call for different services in their lifetime. Unknown to many, such services are actually not part of the bank's core services. They are peripheral and a means for the bank to increase profit. In general, the core services of banks and Building Societies are current accounts, deposit accounts, personal and commercial loans and mortgages. All these services are offered directly by the bank to their clients.

However, many banks are now involved in providing indirect services that are not available within banking proposition, in alliance with main providers of such services. As middlemen, banks offering such services add their margins to the products and services, making it more expensive for many unsuspecting clients. Indirect services of this nature are discretionary portfolio management of stocks and shares, stockbrokerage, unit trusts and Open-Ended Investment Companies (OEICs), life insurance policies, and pension investments. Some banks have now created life assurance unit which they refer to as 'bancassurers. It is important therefore for individuals looking for transactions in those peripheral products and services not to limit their search and interest to their banks alone, but do due diligence to look into the larger market for value for their hard-earned money.

There are actually so many options to choose from. For instance, we have high streets Banks and Building Societies such are Halifax, Barclays, HSBC, Nationwide, Natwest, Satander, Lloyds, etc. In addition to these, the industry has many private banking institutions providing services for different niches of wealthy clients. Such services have deemed added value, and of course come with a bit of premium tag in comparison with what is available on the high streets. It is not uncommon for providers of such services to have a stipulated minimum amount of cash asset for clients to qualify for their services. It must be mentioned that some high streets banks now offer private banking services for their high-net-worth clients. The onus is therefore on you to do your due diligence before settling for any of the institutions, depending on what you are looking for.

-**Life Assurance Companies** – Companies within this group provide insurance services to individuals and corporate organisations via different suitable products. Such services include life insurance, critical illness, income protection, Accident Sickness and Unemployment, Mortgage Protection. Other general insurance services within the sector includes car insurance, home and contents insurance, employers' liability, professional indemnity and many more. Life assurance companies are at liberty to choose their distribution channel. Some may distribute through intermediaries (independent, multi-tied or tied) or develop their own internal sales team.

-Friendly Societies – The origin of Building Societies dated back to the19thcentury. The societies were designed to be a mutual benefits organisation exclusively for their members. The society's asset is used to help members, and there are no shareholders or profit sharing. Due to the self-help nature, the government granted them tax-exempt status, which means their investments and the returns in the hands of investors are not taxed. This makes investing with a Building Society tax-efficient, although there is a prescribed maximum amount that can be invested. Different providers have developed various products around their tax-exempt investments. In addition, they may offer other tax-efficient investments schemes such as Individual Savings Account (ISA). Although they are relevant within the industry, the restrictions due to their tax-exempt status made them small players. However, in 1992, the Friendly Societies Act (1992) was passed which made provision for Building Societies to apply for corporate status and grow their services to include unit trusts/OEICs and ISAs.

-**Multi Products Distributors** – The industry has recently witnessed the distributions of financial services products by companies such as Virgin, Tesco, Marks & Spencer and Post Office, taking advantage of their strong brand positioning and existing clientele base. This was made possible as a result of government's introduction of Charges Access Terms (CAT) Standards. Products that fall within this category do not require professional advice, and therefore can be offered directly to retail clients. Products such as ISA, mortgages, life insurance, Unit Trusts, OEIC's and Pensions that fall within the CAT standard are offered by these companies without requiring due diligence of fact finding or advise. As suitable as this may be for some clients, to some extent, individuals with huge resources to invest may not be inclined to subscribe to over-the-counter investment approach as a means to achieve their financial goals and objectives.

Financial Regulators & Authorities

One of the greatest attractions of UK financial services industry is the regulatory framework. This framework provides protection for investors, thereby boosting consumers' confidence as it affirms their operations within a system with oversight. It is good to know that the government is actively involved in the decision-making process of the regulatory framework through the Treasury Department. The Treasury operates under the direct authority of Chancellor of the Exchequer which is a political office. The chancellor makes policies in line with the party's mandates and manifestoes consisting of promises to the British populace. It is therefore a common thing to see changes in policies depending on which party is in government, thereby making the financial services industry dynamic. When such changes are made, all stakeholders automatically have to review whatever they have put in place.

Although the industry has gone through many regulatory status and changes, the major change was in 1997 which led to the birth of Financial Services Authority (FSA). This body was the only regulatory body of the industry until recently when more changes were made with the introduction of Prudential Regulatory Authority (PRA) and transformation of Financial Services Authority (FSA) to Financial Conduct Authority (FCA). The Prudential Regulatory Authority which is part of Bank of England is UK's regulator of Banks, Building Societies, Credit Unions, insurers and major investment banks. The whole idea behind the reform is part of the relentless efforts of the government to ensure financial stability of the system and market.

The Bank of England is the Central Bank of the United Kingdom. It is the lender of last resort, which means if any of the commercial banks runs into financial difficulties, they can go to Bank of England to borrow money which helps in market liquidity and builds confidence in the system. Other responsibilities of the bank include maintaining monetary and financial stability of the United Kingdom by reviewing and setting the base rate through Monetary Policy Committee on a monthly basis. The base rate is an instrument in the hand of Bank of England to influence demand and inflation. All acts of lending and borrowings in the markets follows the base rate.

Suffice to say that there are other regulators in the industry such as The Pension Regulator (TPR). This body is responsible for the protection of workplace pensions in the UK. They work with employers and Trustees of employer's pension scheme to protect the interest of employees' savings for their old age.

This framework provides protection for investors, thereby boosting consumers' confidence as it affirms their operations within a system with oversight.

The International Stakeholders

The United Kingdom is an international financial centre with participation of firms from all over the globe with diverse financial markets and products. As a result of this, the industry has some international influence. In addition, until recently, United Kingdom was part of European Union (EU) made up of twenty-seven European nations operating free trade in all sectors of their economy among all member states including financial services. As a result, there are international bodies that indirectly have influence in the structure of financial services industry in the United Kingdom. As a matter of fact, due to the union within European states, legislation within the EU supersedes that in the United Kingdom. EU bodies with influence in the UK markets includes European Central Bank, European Supervisory Authorities, European Banking Authority, European Securities and Markets Authority, European Insurance and Occupational Pension Authority, European Systemic Risk Board and European System of Financial Supervisors, until recently when Britain exited the union.

There are other global organisations within the structure but most relevant among them all is the Financial Action Task Force which is the global anti-money laundering task force.

Chapter Action Points

*** Make deliberate efforts to generally understand the system as much as possible.**

*** Locate parts of the system where you would like to be a player.**

*** Find out what is required to benefit from this particular area.**

*** Begin to make plans**

3

BUILDING PERSONAL FINANCIAL PORTFOLIO

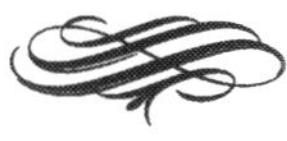

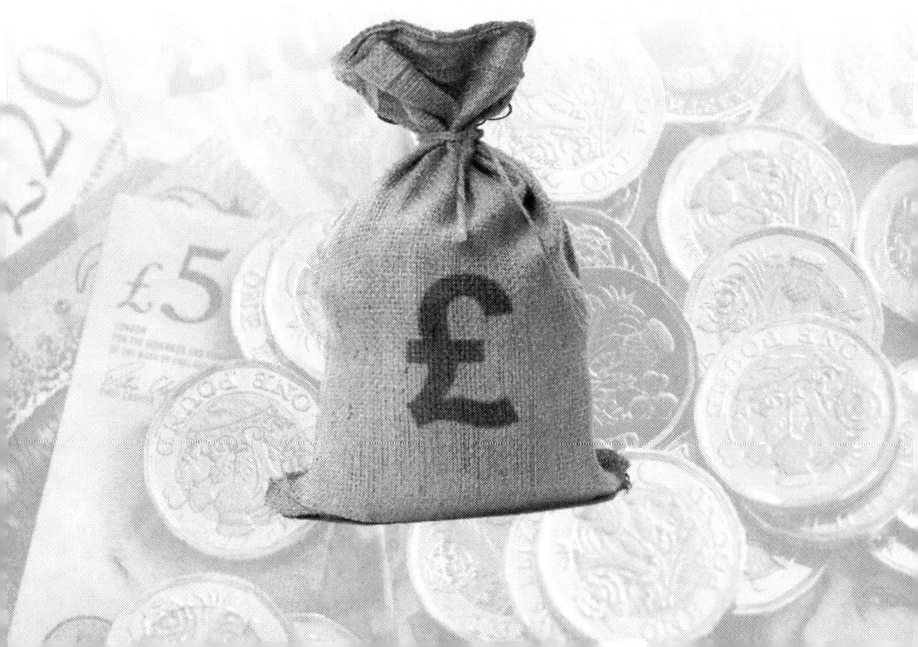

BUILDING PERSONAL FINANCIAL PORTFOLIO

Building personal wealth portfolio requires intentional planning. It doesn't happen by accident. Without proper planning in place, it doesn't matter how much an individual earns, they are likely to still end up in the land of not enough. In my discussions with some of my clients, I have seen professionals who are earning substantial amount of income, and yet are in debt. I have also met individuals on average earnings who have created substantial wealth portfolio through adequate planning. Wealth creation is not about how much you earn but really about what you do with what you earn. Every single pound that comes to your hand has the potential to attract another pound, but it also has the potential to fly away. The good news is that you can determine which direction your money goes through planning.

Let me share with you pivotal information to guide you as you embark on building your wealth portfolio.

Wealth creation is not about how much you earn but really about what you do with what you earn.

When creating a wealth portfolio, I usually like to lay the foundation with some caveats. Firstly, there is no short cut in building a wealth portfolio. The common 'get rich quick syndrome' is a hindrance to many when it comes to investing or building a wealth portfolio. I have met potential investors who wanted their investments to double in twenty-four hours. Unfortunately, their search for such magical returns opens them up to scammers within the industry, who promise them what cannot be delivered or returns that are not sustainable. Building a wealth portfolio requires that individuals have medium to long term investment plan in mind, in line with their attitude to risk and capacity for loss. Looking for overnight returns is a recipe for disappointment.

Secondly, individuals must have a clear vision and objectives for the wealth portfolio. When there is no vision and objectives, there is no restraint and people start well but end up badly. I have had clients who were motivated in starting an investment, but they eventually had many reasons why the funds in the portfolio were used, leaving them with nothing when they needed the resources the most. The most common one has to do with life insurance provisions. Many people find it easy to stop their life insurance arrangements, forgetting the fact that the very risk for which the policy was put in place still exists. A clear understanding of the reason why the policy was put in place i.e., family, protection, mortgage protection, critical illness cover, or income protection must drive any decision about the policy.

Thirdly, it doesn't matter where you are today financially, tomorrow can be better. You may not be able to do anything about yesterday, but you can change your financial position tomorrow by taking actions today. It is always good to start the process of wealth creation as early as possible. Delay always results in loss of opportunity. There is no reason to remain a tenant forever when you have enough resources to service a mortgage and own a property or even properties. As a tenant, your monthly rental payment is helping your landlord to service his or her mortgage borrowing. Generally, rental income is always more than the mortgage payment, therefore leaving extra funds in the pockets of the landlord. The benefit to a landlord is that, while you are living in the property, the value of the property continues to increase, thereby adding value to the landlord's wealth portfolio. This is why it is advisable to act as soon as possible on any area of your financial plans when the resources are available. You cannot do anything about the pasts, but you can take advantage of the present to create a new future.

You cannot do anything about the pasts, but you can take advantage of the present to create a new future.

Fourthly, with wealth creation, only doers really actualise their financial dreams, not hearers. Many have been to financial seminars and workshops, even at a cost. I met a woman who narrated her ordeal in the hands of some self-acclaimed real estate and investments gurus who promised to make her a millionaire within a short period of time. She paid for different programmes and events, and heard so much but did nothing, partly due to her own faults and the unrealistic promises from organisers of the programmes. I strongly advise that you engage only with financial plans that you understand and can implement. The surest way to build wealth portfolio is to act on the information available to you.

Fifthly, how much you know and what you do today will determine how much change you can create for tomorrow. It is important that you have basic understanding of your financial portfolio. Be sure of life insurance arrangement in terms of benefits, sum assured, premiums and terms. Seek advice on what investment schemes you can engage with based on available resources, taking advantage of your tax-efficient annual allowances. A good example is utilising your ISA allowance via stocks and shares in ISA investment portfolio. Be well informed about your mortgage arrangements. If you are currently a tenant, speak with a mortgage broker to know what options are available for you to purchase your own property, and begin to plan towards it. Have basic ideas about your pensions whether its final salary or money purchase. This information is always made available at the point of putting all the plans in place, but people generally don't pay attention to it. You don't have to be an expert, but basic knowledge would give you a vivid picture of what tomorrow would look like financially. It is motivating when you can see a better future in the present.

Lastly, l strongly advice that you seek financial advice to support your financial plans. Having professional advice goes a long way in a complex industry like the financial services in the United Kingdom. The industry is systemised and full of products and services designed to help different individuals with different profiles to achieve their financial plans and goals. Identifying the most suitable and valuable for you as an investor often requires more than 'do it yourself'. For example, how would you know the most suitable mortgage for you out of the several thousands of products available on the market with different features and criteria put in place by the lender? How can you identify which life insurance provider has better critical illness conditions and good claim payment record and administrative services? How would you determine a suitable investment portfolio for yourself and select the funds? All these require due diligence from a professional financial adviser, who is qualified and authorised to provide advisory services in those areas. Although seeking professional advice involves paying charges, but the value far exceeds the fees. All the work from beginning to the end is done for you, your adviser is available to assist, make clarifications and ensure you are on the right path to achieve your financial goals.

Maximising the System

Earlier in this book, I emphasised the fact that the financial services industry in the United Kingdom is systemised. It is pretty much the case in other developed nations. The reason is because the economy of such nations thrives on the dynamism of the industry. The sector has consistently been the largest contributor to the economic output; therefore, the government invests a lot of effort to ensure the sector is dynamic and attractive to investors at home and globally through their policies. So, many international investors find United Kingdom a comfortable place to invest.

In response to government policies, the market players constantly introduce new products and services to suit investors and to enable them maximise investment opportunities. Now, to maximise these opportunities within the system, investors must have plans and objectives.

Financial Plans and Objectives – every individual should have detailed financial plans and objectives to help them know how to deploy available resources, be it regular contributions or lump sum. If you are a salary earner, be intentional about creating wealth by having a budget for it in your monthly income. This has nothing to do with the level of income, but rather prioritising the desired future in the present. Being intentional means running a budget that accommodates your financial plans and goals regardless of your level of income. Sometimes, we may have to deny ourselves of certain privileges today in order to reach the set goals for the future. For example, an individual that wants to get on the property ladder and requires some amount of capital as deposit will have to put funds aside over a period of time to build capital from the regular income. Setting such a goal and following through may require denying yourself of some immediate pleasures, but the joy of acquiring your own home far exceeds the pain of the sacrifice.

Parents who want to leave a legacy of funds in any unforeseen event of death must make provision for life insurance with lump sum benefit as part of their plan, to be paid to their survivors in any event of earlier death. They can also use such provision as a tool for wealth transfer to the next generation whenever death occurs. Individuals desiring to have a good retirement life must plan how to build required capital to fund income at retirement when they are no longer earning an income. Without clear plans in mind, it is difficult to create a wealth portfolio.

Being intentional means running a budget that accommodates your financial plans and goals regardless of your level of income.

SEEKING PROFESSIONAL FINANCIAL PLANNING ADVICE

Although I have mentioned severally the advantages of seeking professional financial advice in creating a personal financial portfolio and building wealth, I would like to reiterate its importance in achieving your financial objectives in a safe and confident manner in comparison to self-attempt. There is nothing wrong with self-attempts, provided you are equipped with adequate knowledge to make the right decision and have the time to manage what you have put in place through close monitoring.

Be that as it may, in my meetings with individuals who adopted the *'do-it-yourself'* approach, when asked how they came about the investment decisions they have made so far, the most popular answer that I get is that somebody did it and they felt it would be good for them also, but they later realised it is not what they thought. Next to that answer is that someone introduced the investment to them and they bought into it, only to realise it is not really for them. Painfully, many of these individuals will continue to propagate negative campaign about such products, until they see someone who can educate them that the product itself may not be bad, but it is just not suitable to meet their needs and objectives.

For example, I have met people who said Individual Savings Account (ISA) is not good, because they put money into it for years and didn't get anything back. Surprisingly, looking deeper into their complaints, l discovered that their fund was sitting in Cash ISA in a low interest environment. Of course, they will get next to nothing in returns. What many don't know is that there is investment ISA and the return on it far exceeds the stipends from Cash ISA funds. This doesn't mean that Cash ISA is not good, but it wasn't suitable for their investment objectives. They did not know this early enough because they failed to seek advice.

Aside from this, I have also met people trying to figure out whether their mortgage should be structured as capital repayment or interest only. Some have argued that one is better than the other on both sides of the isles. However, both types are products designed to be suitable for different individuals with different circumstances and different financial objectives. The same thing applies to life insurance and pension arrangements. Many have missed out a great deal of opportunities by turning down pension provisions from their employers because they did not want any deductions from their salaries. They were blind to the fact that the free money from their employers' contributions is building up investments for them to fund a better lifestyle for them in their old age. Some are ignorant of the tax-relief advantages in pension investments while some have the notion that they may not get their money back at old-age.

I have interacted with clients who won't put life insurance in place for family protection or otherwise, mainly because they are not comfortable with the thought of not getting anything back at the end of the term if no death or critical illness occurs.

The above and many more are the reasons why individuals are better off seeking professional advice in creating their wealth portfolios.

SECTION TWO

INTRODUCTION

PILLARS OF WEALTH CREATION IN THE UNITED KINGDOM

In this section, we will examine the four major pillars of wealth creation in the United Kingdom. These four major areas are the pillars of the economy as well as that of the industry, but most importantly are the components of individuals financial portfolio. These four pillars are: -

*Mortgages
*Investments
*Life Insurance
*Pensions

MORTGAGES

In the United Kingdom, majority of families owned their properties. According to the House of Commons Library publication of 9th June 2017 on "Home Ownership and Renting: Demographics",

"At the end of 2016, around 65% of UK households were owner-occupiers, 17% were renting from a private landlord and 18% were renting from a social landlord. Social renting has declined since 1996, while private renting has increased. The rate of owner-occupation is also slightly lower than it was ten years ago".

The culture of residential properties is that of a mixture of ownership with that of renting. From the above report, it could be considered that the country has a significant level of owner occupier however in comparison with other European countries, it may be considered as low in comparison with a record homeowner of 96% in Romanian. Majority of European countries have a record of as much as 70% owner occupier. In most of these European countries, owning your own property is made possible through access to mortgage borrowing. According to Council of Mortgage Lenders in their 2016 report, there are 11.1 million mortgaged properties with a total mortgage borrowing of £1.3 Trillion. The report further says 83.3% of those were homeowners while 16.7% were buy-to-let. This further reinforces the culture of owner occupier in the country alongside investment opportunities for residential landlords through buy-to-let properties. It is therefore common for

UK residents to desire to own their properties as soon as they can afford it most especially when the financial services industry provides bulk of resources needed through mortgage borrowing.

In very simple terms, a mortgage is a loan of money you get from the bank or building society to buy a house. The property therefore automatically becomes the collateral for the borrowing which means the mortgage borrowing is secured on the property. If anything happens and the borrower could not repay the mortgage, the lender owns the legal right to repossess the property and sell to recover the borrowed funds. The borrowing will come with interest to be paid within a stipulated period referred to as mortgage term.

> *"At the end of 2016, around 65% of UK households were owner-occupiers, 17% were renting from a private landlord and 18% were renting from a social landlord.*

Mortgage Interest Rates

The interest rates on mortgages are primarily dictated by the Bank of England interest rates. The Bank of England interest rates is an instrument the bank uses to control monetary policy. They bank therefore makes adjustments to interest rates as they deemed fit to achieve their set objectives of inflationary rate within their set economic policy. Changes in rates therefore by the bank tends to influence mortgage interest rates available in the market. It is therefore a common practice in the industry to envisage clients' capability to service their mortgage borrowing if in any event there's an increase in interest rates. To protect clients, most especially first-time buyers, advisers do recommend fixed rates products to ensure that stability in clients budgeting. A fixed rates mortgage product guarantees that rates will remain the same for the fixed periods regardless of changes by Bank of England. Take for example if Mr Jones obtained a mortgage product from XYZ Bank with following details – **"A fixed rate of 1.44% until 02 January 2023"**, Mr Jones will only pay an interest of 1.44% on his borrowing till 2nd of July 2023 regardless of increase or decrease in Bank of England rate during this period. In a period of increasing interest rates, Mr Jones will be at advantage not paying more that 1.44% on his borrowing. However, the case is reversed in a period of decreasing rates as he would not be able to benefit from the rates either as he's on a fixed rate mortgage product.

After a period of fixed rates, his mortgage borrowing will revert to lender's standard variable, rate usually higher than the initial rate. At this point Mr Jones need to decide whether he will continue to keep his mortgage borrowing with existing lender or look for a cheaper rate with another lender to keep his mortgage cost down. The most important thing to consider at this point is whether there's any penalty attached to his mortgage redemption at on-set, and cost of the impact in comparison with the benefits of the new products available. Most mortgage products will have early redemption penalty attached to it. The lenders do this to protect themselves from losing out on their cost of sourcing for mortgage funds for borrowers should they decide to leave and take their mortgage elsewhere. The Early Repayment Charges will be a percentage of the amount of money borrowed and may be fixed through the fixed period or decreases as the fixed period progresses. Detailed information about interest rates terms and conditions are contained in personalised illustration of mortgage products called Key Facts Illustration which must be given to all mortgage clients at the initial stage of mortgage processing. There are other types of interest rates in the market in addition to fixed and variable rates. Without going into details the list includes the following – discounted rates, tracker rates, capped rates, collar rates, Libor rates.

Mortgage Term

The mortgage term is the number of years it will take the borrower to pay back the amount borrowed back to the lender. Typically, twenty five years however it could be more or less depending on the age of the borrower and level of affordability of repayment. Younger borrowers may have ample number of years to retirement thereby able to stretch their mortgage terms beyond the customary twenty-five years, making their repayment more affordable, compared with an older individual close to retirement. The whole idea from lenders and industry perspectives is that your mortgage should be paid off by your retirement age. Lending beyond retirement therefore will require a proof of income at your retirement age to demonstrate that after your retirement you will still have sufficient level of income to service your mortgage borrowing. Some lenders may not be comfortable with lending beyond client's retirement age. However, in the recent times, we now have products lending till the age of seventy.

Your mortgage term can be adjusted in line with your financial status at your mortgage review sessions. The whole idea is to ensure you are comfortable with your repayment and at the same time able to maximise available resources. Individuals with increase in their level of income with surplus disposable income may consider increasing monthly repayment by decreasing the term. The logic behind such action is to pay off the mortgage earlier than scheduled to reduce the amount of interest payable on the borrowing. Individuals with less income may consider increasing the term of mortgage to accommodate his current level of affordability subject to approval by the lender.

Types of Mortgages

Mortgage borrowing can be structured in two ways. These

are: - Capital Repayment (Repayment Mortgage) or Interest Only.

***Capital Repayment (Repayment Mortgage)–** The mortgage is structured to continually reduce the capital borrowing on monthly basis in addition to paying interest. Therefore, every monthly repayment is a combination of part of capital borrowed and monthly interest due on the outstanding borrowing. At the initial phase of the mortgage most of the monthly repayment goes towards interest repayment. A borrower may not begin to see reduction in the amount of capital borrowed until later part of the mortgage. At every mortgage anniversary, provider will forward a mortgage statement to borrower with information about their mortgage repayments throughout the year and how much their new repayment will be for the year ahead. However, the mortgage is structured in such a way that it will be repaid off at the end of the mortgage term as long as the borrower commits to the repayment plan without default. For borrowers with low-risk appetite who wants a guarantee that his mortgage will be paid off by the end of the term, this will be a suitable type of mortgage. Other benefit of this type of mortgage is that it helps borrowers to build up equity on their property quicker than Interest-Only mortgage. They also pay less gross interest rate as their outstanding borrowing decreases every year allowing them to save a bit of money. Suffice to say that the monthly repayment of this type of mortgage will be greater than that of corresponding interest-only mortgage. Most family residence mortgages are structured on capital repayment basis as most parents desires to leave a debt-free home for their survivors. Other benefit of capital repayment mortgage is the equity on the property, which is a form of savings and investments which can always be released for further investments when required. The graph below shows the dynamics of capital repayment mortgage.

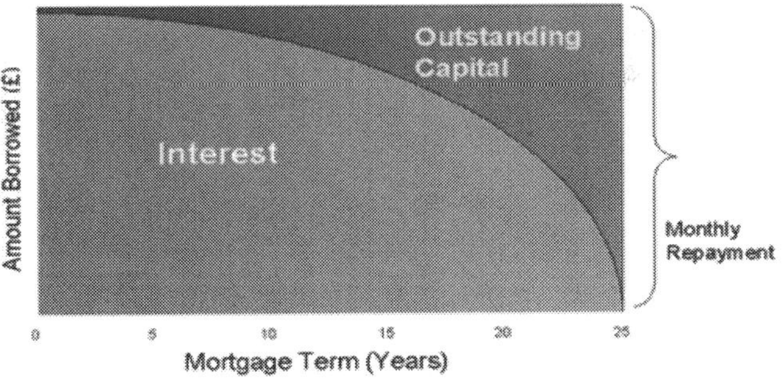

Fig 1 – *Capital Repayment Mortgage*

Other benefits of this type of mortgage is that it helps borrowers to build up equity on their property quicker than Interest-Only mortgage

***Interest Only** – With this type of mortgage the monthly repayment consists only of interest due on the borrowing only, therefore the capital borrowing remains the same throughout the mortgage term. The capital is expected to be repaid fully at the end of the mortgage term. Borrowers are expected to put investment provision in place which can be used to offset the capital borrowing at the end of the term. Such investments could be a contributions into a collective investment schemes via Unit Trusts, OEIC's or ISA looking for growth opportunities. In the time past it was an endowment policies investment which unfortunately recorded great shortfalls leading to huge mis-selling claims within the industry as borrowers' complaint they have no knowledge of how the investment works. The risk still exists with contributions via any of the collectives mentioned above as there's no guarantee with such investment performance. "Investors may get more or less than the amount invested" is a compulsory caveat that must be documented in all illustrative paper works given to investors by their financial advisers. It is therefore advisable for any individual with low-risk appetite with desire to have his mortgage borrowing fully paid at the end to abstain from this type of mortgage arrangement most especially when arranging for main residence mortgage.

At the end of the mortgage term when lenders demand for redemption of their money, the borrower either have enough funds to pay off the mortgage or sell the property and pay the lenders funds and keep the rest as capital gains on the property. The challenge however is if the property is the main residence for the family, such an arrangement creates problem of accommodation for the family. The family will have to look for another property to buy with whatever amount is left after payment of outstanding mortgage on the property. The good news is that there's no capital gain tax liability at the sale of main residence.

The case is different if the property is an investment property due to tax implications. After all expenses paid, the remainder of the gains is liable to Capital Gains Tax. No capital gain tax is payable on main residence. The table below shows the dynamics of Interest-Only mortgage during the term.

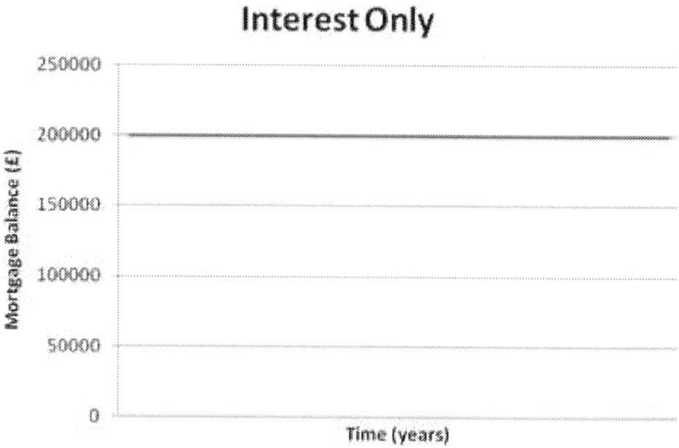

Fig 2 – *Interest-Only Mortgage*

It is therefore advisable for any individual with low-risk appetite with desire to have his mortgage borrowing fully paid at the end to abstain from this type of mortgage arrangement most especially when arranging for main residence mortgage.

Other Mortgage Types

Having gone through the two major types of mortgage arrangement, there are diverse mortgage products with different features created by the industry to increase consumers choice and competition. Let's now examine some other mortgages products:-

***Cashback Mortgages –** With this type of mortgage the lender designed the products with a promise of giving a certain amount of money back to the borrower at the completion of the mortgage. This is a typical marketing incentive that must be looked at carefully to ensure that such incentive is not disadvantageous with higher rates and other conditions. A cashback mortgage will be attractive to mortgage buyers needing money to move after mortgage completion.

***Offset Mortgages** – The concept of Offset mortgage is the interaction of borrowers' savings and mortgage account together. At the end of every month the lender will deduct the amount of funds available from the outstanding mortgage borrowing to determine the interest to be paid that month. For example – "Janine has an Offset Mortgage account with outstanding borrowing of £150,000 this month. She's also got £15,000 in her savings account. At the end of the month lender will deduct the £15,000 from the £150,000 and calculate interest on £135,000". Janine can still access her savings account to draw funds if she wants to but the more, she offsets the mortgage, the lesser the amount of interest paid and the quicker she can pay off her mortgage. It must be noted that when you use your savings to offset your mortgage, no interest will be earned on your savings. However, no tax will be paid which makes it to be tax-efficient for higher rate and additional rate taxpayers. This type of mortgage therefore is ideal for individuals with huge savings account and higher rate taxpayers.

***Flexible Mortgages –** The attractive feature of this type of mortgage is the ability to make overpayments, underpayments or even take payment holiday if required. Borrowers who envisage instability in their income will be attracted to this type of mortgage. Contract workers with void period before new contracts may consider this type of mortgage arrangements.

***First-Time Buyer Mortgage –** This type of mortgages are exclusive for first time buyers only. It's typical that the deposit required will be lower in comparison with borrowers buying another home or moving their mortgage or buying for investment purposes.

***Buy-to-Let (BTL)** – As the name implies, the mortgage is designed for those who wants to buy and rent the property out collecting rental income from tenants. The projected rental income is therefore part of the affordability calculations. Landlords within the BTL sector are now been classified as amateurs and professionals depending on the number of properties within their buy-to-let portfolio. Individuals with less than five properties are referred to as amateurs while more than five are referred to as professionals. Although it is debatable whether the number of properties in a portfolio alone should be the criteria to qualify landlords as professional or amateur. This will be attended to with more details in my mortgage hand book.

STEPS TO PROPERTY LADDER

Understanding the process of buying a home in the United Kingdom is very important for a first-time buyer. Because a lot of decisions making is involved, it is always advisable for buyers to be well informed about the process. Truth be told, there's always that joy of looking forward to owning a house when making efforts to buy a property but individuals must not allow their emotions to override doing their due diligence about the process. The following steps are essentials in the process of buying a house: -

Step One:

Determine your maximum purchase price.

This step is an important prerequisite to all other steps in buying a property most especially when you are using a mortgage for your purchase. It is important that you know how much mortgage you can get from the market and how much you have as your deposit. If you are using any of the government schemes in addition, you need to know how much scheme funding you are getting. The combination of mortgage from lender plus your deposit and any government scheme funding, if applicable will determine maximum amount of purchase price you can afford.

In determining the maximum amount they can lend you, the lender will put into consideration all your existing financial commitments such loans, higher purchase, credit cards, maintenance cost, monthly bills on energy, and any essential expenditure before arriving at final lending figure. Although the lender will offer a figure they can lend, you also must take into consideration your other expenses that could impede your monthly expenditure to decide whether you want that much or less to ensure affordability of servicing your mortgage without default. It's always a good decision to ensure you are not working on tight rope to pay your mortgage every month.

I recommend buyers seek the help of Financial or Mortgage adviser before they start looking for properties. Not only will this help them to know how much they can borrow, but the adviser may also help with having an Agreement in Principle in place. An Agreement or Decision in Principle (AIP or DIP) is a promissory agreement by the lender to borrow the buyer an agreed sum of money for their purchase subject to final satisfactory underwriting. A crucial point that must be noted is that processing an AIP may involves credit search of the applicant. Some lenders will conduct full credit check while others claim to conduct partial credit check initially, and full check during full application. The underwriting procedure will require that the borrower produce documentation to support their purchase and to conduct all necessary checks and be satisfied. Such documentation includes but not limited to payslips, P60,bank statements, Self-Assessment returns (SA302) and Tax Year Overview for self-employed individuals, Proof of address, Photo identification document (Passport or Driver's license) etc. Mortgage underwriters sometimes do ask for additional documents to support mortgage applications depending on the nature of the application itself.

I recommend buyers seek the help of Financial or Mortgage adviser before they start looking for properties. Not only will this help them to know how much they can borrow, but the adviser may also help with having an Agreement in Principle in place.

Step Two:
Searching for Properties

This is one of the interesting aspect of the purchase process. After you have decided your purchase price range, the search for property begins. In searching for your ideal property, it is advisable to have a listed features of what you want in your property. This will help guide your search and maximise your time. You do not want to view every property available just to discover you don't like those properties as they do not fit into your ideal home. Traditionally, local estate agents are the best sources of registering your purchase interest as most sellers local to your location must have registered their interest to sell with the local agents. However, technology has amplified the opportunities for both buyers and sellers to use estate agents not necessarily local to them. It's now a common trend for buyers to find their ideal property through online estate agents rather than local agents.

Other sources of searching for your ideal property is through local papers of where you want to buy. Many estate agents advertise their property stocks on weekly basis for buyers to see. It's advisable to find one local agent and discuss details of your ideal property. The reason is because, in addition to taking you through their current stock of property similar to your ideal home, they will keep you updated of any new instruction just coming to the market which may be suitable for you. Although you have a listed feature of an ideal property, you must prepare your mind to make some compromise as most properties you will view were built without your listed features in mind. Some features will be more important than others, therefore know what you can do without. As soon as you find a suitable property, the next step for you is to make an offer.

Step Three:

Making an Offer

Making an offer for your purchase will be easy if you have decided your purchase range and possibly with an

Agreement in Principe in hand. You will need to let the estate agent know how much you are willing to pay for the property. Knowing how much you are willing to pay requires your due diligence of knowing the average price for your kind of property in the neighbourhood. One error you must avoid is paying too much for the going price in your neighbourhood. You must note that the estate agent is not working for you but rather for the seller. The seller pays the agent to sell the property and an agreed percentage of the sales price goes to the estate agent as sales commission. It is therefore in estate agents best interest to sell the property as high as possible. They also like to sell as quickly as possible.

One error you must avoid is paying too much for the going price in your neighbourhood.

You also need to note that most sellers expect buyers to offer below the advertised price, therefore your offer will be below the advertised price. The agent will present your offer to the seller and come back to you if your offer is acceptable or not. If your offer is declined, you can increase your offer, if it's still within the going range in the neighbourhood and still covered by your purchase range. Once your offer has been accepted, the next step in your buying process is to make full mortgage application.

Step Four:
Mortgage Application

Now that you've made an offer and the offer has been accepted, you can return to your financial adviser with details of property and other documents required by the lender to support your mortgage application for adviser to submit a full mortgage application. Supporting documents for full mortgage application varies from lender to lender but generically the following are likely to future in documents required for underwriting purposes:-

*Contract or Employment letter
*Pay Slips
*P60
*Bank Statements
*Audited Accounts (if self-employed)
*Self Assessment Returns (SA302)
*Tax Year Overview
*Photo Identification Document (Passport or Driver's License)
*Proof of Address – Utility Bill, Council Tax,

Lenders have discretion to ask for as much information as possible to support their underwriting decision. A full credit check is involved during mortgage application processing. It is advisable for applicants to ensure their credit report is in good shape before making commitment to full mortgage application. If in doubt, applicant can obtain a copy of their credit reports from Experian or Equifax. The credit report will help the adviser also to determine which lender is willing to provide mortgage lending based on the content of applicant's credit report. This is important because, some lenders are happy to lend to adverse applicants while other are not. Therefore, an upfront knowledge of credit status will help the adviser and applicants to know their fate before progressing with mortgage application.

Having submitted the mortgage application with all required documents, the underwriting process by the lender will commence and most lenders will update advisers about the progress of their application from time to time. If they need further information, they will let the adviser know.

It is advisable for applicants to ensure their credit report is in good shape before making commitment to full mortgage application.

Step Five:
Property Valuation
It's always a good sign when lenders instruct valuation of the property. It simply means they are willing to offer the mortgage as long as the valuation is in line with submitted purchased price. Property valuation is conducted by qualified valuers at the expense of the applicant. However, l should mention that there are occasional lender's incentives in form of free valuation, which means lenders are responsible for valuation cost. The lenders valuation is basic for them to ascertain the value of the collateral before releasing the fund. However, applicants may instruct more advanced valuation

(Full Home Survey or Home Buyers) reports with additional costs for own advantage. Such a report may help to identify hidden problems in the property which can be used as a negotiating tool with the seller to reduce the purchase price. The valuation report will take into consideration the state of the property, location, size, and neighbourhood, proximity to amenities, current market conditions and ease of sale in future.

If lenders have any concern with the outcome of the report in terms of state of property or value they may decide not to lend or reduce the amount of lending. If there's no such concern and the valuation comes out with expected price range, lender may progress to offer. Depending on the type of property that applicant is buying, other cases that can lead to mortgage decline are:

*Freehold flats
*Short Leasehold Properties – Usually less than 60
*Properties with structural defects
*Properties with unclear shared areas

It is good to know that most mortgage lenders now have a panel of qualified valuers they use for their mortgage valuation and they may not allow any valuer outside of their panel to do valuation for their mortgage cases.

Step Six:

Mortgage Offer

A satisfactory valuation outcome normally leads to lender issuing a formal mortgage offer to applicant. Offer letters come with a valid date. Therefore, the offer must be exercised before the expiration of the date. Most lenders expect completion of mortgage within a period of ninety days. If for any reason the mortgage is not completed within this period, renewal of offer is at lender's discretion. The formal offer letter contains all terms and conditions of offer including details of the mortgage products. In some instances, the offer letter may contain some conditions attached to it. Applicants must ensure they fully understand the contents of their offer letter before they progress to the next phase of their mortgage process which is the onset of legal commitments to the process.

Step Seven

Mortgage Conveyancing

Conveyancing is the legal procedure through which a seller transfers the right of ownership to the buyer. The procedure involves a lot of legal frameworks that applicants are advised to employ the service of solicitors or qualified conveyancer to conduct the process. Lenders may insist that applicant must choose from their panel of solicitors of approved conveyancer, or they may have liberty to choose their own legal representative. There are occasions where the lenders offer free conveyancing therefore lender's conveyancer or solicitor will do all the legal work.

The conveyancing work includes the following:

*Settlement and Transfer process

*Protecting client's legal right

*Exchange of contracts
*Financial transaction between buyer and seller
*Registering Title Deed
*Local Searches on Property
*Completion of Sales

Additional works are involved if the purchase is a Leasehold property as against a Freehold property. With a leasehold property, the buyer owns the property but not the land. The leaseholder owns the land and therefore will charge land rent. The conveyancer needs to be sure that the terms of lease are suitable and understood by the applicant. Other charges with a leasehold property such as service charge must be made known to the applicant at this stage. It's for all these reasons that is always advisable to employ qualified legal professional to represent a buyer rather than do it yourself. Both buyers and seller's legal representative will communicate on behalf of their clients and agree exchange and completion date subject to satisfactory outcome of their searches and other administrative steps. As soon as both parties are satisfied, they can set the completion date which is the day the buyer takes up the ownership of the property.

Step Eight:
Mortgage Completion.
Hurray!!! This is the day the applicant's picks up the key to his new home and becomes the legal owner of the property. This is the day that the purchase price paid by the buyer is transferred to the seller's solicitor who will forward to the

seller. From this date the countdown to your mortgage years and monthly repayment commences. From that day you are now the bonafide owner of the property and you are responsible for everything that happens in the property i.e. gas bills, electricity, water, council tax, etc.

Costs Associated with Mortgage

*Deposit – You deposit is the amount of money you are putting towards the purchase of your property. Although we have witnessed in time past 100% mortgage borrowing, such products have since disappeared after the global recession triggered by irresponsible borrowing by lenders which triggered the recession. The market have since employed the culture of due diligence and responsible borrowing, therefore the buyer must have some amount of money to put towards the purchase. The amount of your deposit is dependent on the mortgage product available. For example, if the mortgage product is 90% Loan to Value (9% LTV), your deposit towards your borrowing will be 10% of your purchase price.

*Let's assume Mr Jones is making a purchase of a property valued for £300,000 with a mortgage product of 90% LTV, his deposit for this purchase will be £30,000 while the lender will lend a sum of £270,000 towards the purchase. Deposit may be from your savings from income or gifts from different sources. In the recent times it's become a common thing for buyers to benefit from the bank of mum and dad as source of deposit, as many could not safe enough money for deposit due to property prices that kept going up.

*Arrangement Fee–Arrangement fee is the fee charged by the lender for arranging the mortgage for you. This fee is usually a certain percentage of your mortgage borrowing and you have the option of paying this money upfront or adding it to your mortgage borrowing. The advantage of paying upfront if you can afford it is that you save yourself mortgage interest on that bit if added to your borrowing. Also adding this sum to your borrowing will increase your loan to value amount and could lead to product decline on some rare instances.

*Advisory Fee – Depending on how you source your mortgage, using mortgage adviser may involve payment of advisory fee. The mortgage adviser will let their client know upfront if there's any fee to be paid. It is also advisable that clients ask their adviser the cost of advise upfront if applicable. Advisers may charge a certain percentage of amount of borrowing or a flat fee arrangement for every mortgage application. It is part of regulatory and compliance practice for advisers to disclose their charges as soon as they meet with client.

*Legal Fee – Legal fee is the charges made by your solicitor or conveyancer to do all legal works of your property purchase as detailed above. Interestingly charges varies from one firm to the other therefore there's no set amount. It is good for buyers to shop around for value if they have the liberty to do.

*Valuation Fee–Lenders always want to ensure that the value of the property is in line with the amount of money they are lending. As part of their due diligence, they will instruct a professional value to do a valuation albeit at the cost of the borrower as explained above.

*Stamp Duty – This is the government tax on the purchase of property. It is referred to as Stamp Duty Land Tax (SDLT). The tax is payable on purchase of property or lands. In Scotland it's called Land and Building Transaction Tax. Over the years the government has made several changes to tax payable when purchasing a property depending on type of buyer and purpose of purchase. With effect from 22nd November 2017, first-time buyers buying their first home no longer have to pay stamp duty land tax over property with a value up to £300,000. A tax charge of 5% applies between £300,001 and

£500,000 under this new government rules made known in Budget 2017. Prior to this time, SDLT payable on purchase of properties are as detailed below:-

SDLT Table

Property Value	SDLT Rate
Up to £125,000	Zero
The next £125,000 (the portion from £125,001 to £250,000)	2%
The next £675,000 (the portion from £250,001 to £925,000)	5%
The next £575,000 (the portion from £925,001 to £1.5 million)	10%
The remaining amount (the portion above £1.5 million)	12%

Fig 3 – *Stamp Duty Land Tax*

It must be noted that higher rates of 3% applies to people buying additional residential properties for letting. You will not have to pay the 3% in a case of replacing your old property for a new one as long as the old property has been sold. It must be noted that if you haven't sold your old property before buying the new one, you will have to pay the 3% higher rates for additional property. However, you may get a refund if you sell your old property within thirty-six months of your new purchase.

For non-residential properties and lands the calculation of SDLT is similar to the above but different rates and threshold. Initial tax relief is granted up to a value of £150,000 followed by 2% on value between £150,001 to

£250,000 and 5% £250,000 and above. Buyer's solicitor will take them through the tax liability as part of the conveyancing process.

*Insurance Costs–Most lenders will not release funds for purchase until a building insurance is in place to ensure that the risk of property damages is protected as this is the collateral for their capital. Buyers therefore are compelled to pay a premium for building insurance from onset of their property purchase. Individuals may add contents insurance to protect their assets against theft or damage within the property. In addition to building and content insurance, it is highly recommended and advisable that borrowers have life insurance policy in place to cover their mortgage borrowing. Life insurance policy protects the borrower and their families against unforeseen event of death or earlier diagnosis of critical illness condition. It is also highly recommended that borrowers consider income protection policy to protect their income against ill health which may affect them from carrying out their occupation for a very long time.

*Other Costs–Other miscellaneous costs that must be considered when moving homes includes removal costs, re-directory costs, minor refurbishing and installations of new fixtures etc. All these sometimes could pile up to major costs most especially when moving into old properties.

The whole idea of this chapter and section is to give a layman a generic overview of mortgage process. Hope we have been able to achieve that so far. A case study of a first-time buyer is hereby included to highlight some of the issues raised in mortgage processing above.

Niyi Murele is a 32-year-old IT Consultant with a gross income of £70,000 per annum. He's currently a tenant in a rented accommodation paying £1,500 per month. He's now processing a mortgage to purchase a property valued for £250,000. He's saved as much £50,000 for his deposit and other costs. His Financial Adviser confirmed he will be able to get mortgage product of 90% loan to value with a 25 year term and initial 2.21% fixed rate product for a period of 2 years and variable rate of 3.95% thereafter. The mortgage product comes with an arrangement fee of £999 which can be added to the loan or pay upfront if he chooses to. Niyi is responsible for valuation fee and legal fee. The Key Features Information of Niyi's mortgage product is at Appendix 1

It is advisable for an individual to get on property ladder as soon as they have the means and opportunity to do so. The strong investment argument behind this is the fact that during rental years, part of the monthly rent could have served as savings as the capital borrowing reduces. Secondly the value of the property itself continues to grow progressively. As a tenant, not only do you help the landlords to pay their mortgage, at the end of your tenancy you leave empty handed without sharing any benefit of increase in equity of the property.

It is advisable for an individual to get on property ladder as soon as they have the means and opportunity to do so.

Let's consider Niyi Murele above as a good example. Assuming he's rented his present accommodation for five years with a monthly rent of £1,500. In five years, he's paid out a total sum of £90,000 to his landlord. Properties appreciates by up to 7% a year in the United Kingdom. The value of the property must have gone up by up to 35% to the benefit of the landlord only. When he leaves this property, he leaves with nothing. As a matter of fact, the landlord will insists that he puts the property in good condition otherwise he may not get his deposit back. It's for these reasons and many more that l recommend that subject to affordability individuals living in the United Kingdom are better off owning their homes than renting.

Chapter Action Points

*Purpose to own your property from now if you are currently renting.

*Give yourself time-frame for purchase and start a savings plan towards your deposit if you haven't one in place already.

*If you already own your property, consider building investment property portfolio by raising capital on your current property for new purchase.

*Seek professional advice of how to achieve capital raising and new purchase.

*Constantly review your existing property portfolio to ensure you have value for your money.

LIFE INSURANCE

LIFE INSURANCE

Life Insurance is a very important aspect of financial planning for individuals and family. Generally, it is a way of ensuring peace of mind in case of any unforeseen circumstances that could jeopardise the financial well-being of a family and affect their quality of living. As individuals go through the stages of life, there are some risks at different phases, which if unprepared for, can hinder them and/or their and family from achieving their financial and life goals. Such risks include among many death, sickness, disability, critical illness, unemployment, etc. As part of planning for a wealthy future therefore, individuals must take into consideration things that can frustrate their plans and find means of making adequate provisions for such. Apart from having more than enough capital in cash, the alternative way is to put life insurance in place to cater for any of these events if it happens along the journey of life.

Life insurance needs will differ from one individual to the other as our financial objectives are different also. However, broadly within the concepts of 'Life Cycles', there are generic factors that induce the protection priorities of individuals and their families. The Life Cycle can be split into three phases, which are – The Vulnerable Phase, The Relaxing Phase and The Anxious Phase.

The Vulnerable Phase

The Vulnerable Phase of life is the early years which are characterised by marriage or relationship and starting out a family. Prior to this time, the two individuals were single without any dependant. Their only need at that stage was for themselves, but now they are together and dependent on each other. The household expenditure may be on two sets of incomes or only one. The family grows as children come and so dependency in this family grows also. The couple have now taken out a mortgage with a term of up to twenty-five years or more. This probably will be the biggest financial liability of their lifetime. There is need to make protection provision for the children till their independent age, and also for the family at large against death of either of the parents or prolonged or critical illness that could affect family income.

The Relaxing Phase

The Relaxing Phase sets in as individuals step into their of 40s. Most couples are more settled at this stage and probably have more income in comparison with the Vulnerable Phase. Their children have probably now come of age and are looking towards financial independence. There is the possibility that couples have more money to save and less need for protection. However, there could be an increase in life cover against death to guarantee the new standard of living and also increase in level of income protection to guarantee new level of earnings. At this stage also, couples may be adding new policies for health care and provision for long term care in future.

The Anxious Phase

This last phase in life cycle is very significant. As people enter 50s and beyond, generally their life experiences begin to change. They are coming to the peak of their working life and now confronted with reality of retirement in not too long a distance of time. The thought of life after retirement will be part of their daily meditation. At this stretch of age, they begin to see friends and people of similar age dying or become ill. Possibly their children are now financially independent by now. However, there is almost no time to fund pensions to desired level if for any reason there is a huge shortfall. The thought of long-term care will filter through their minds from time to time. For some who have built substantial estate, the thought of estate planning will be of concern to ensure that estates are passed to the next generation in a very tax-efficient way.

Generally, it is a way of ensuring peace of mind in case of any unforeseen circumstances that could jeopardise the financial well-being of a family and affect their quality of living.

These phases of life must be given consideration in your wealth creation plans with adequate provisions made to ensure that the risks that are involved at every facet are well covered. As previously mentioned, the most conventional way of mitigating the risks is by putting suitable life insurance policies in place.

Key Factors Influencing Insurance

There are key factors that are the influencers of suitable provisions for insurance policy for individuals or family. They are: -

*Financial Liabilities
*Age
*Existing Provision (work or otherwise)
*Dependants
*Level of Income
*Legacy

Financial Liabilities – These are financial commitments and obligation on the couple as a result of borrowing for one reason or the other. For example, if the couple have raised a mortgage borrowing to fund their property purchase, the repayment of such liability may have been structured to stretch over two decades. This simply means there is a risk over that property for that period of time, if anything happens that can affect their ability to service their mortgage borrowing. Usually, lenders warn borrowers upfront that their house may be repossessed if they are unable to service the mortgage. It is therefore important that borrowers make provisions for all those risks that can affect their mortgage repayment. Incidences in household that can affect their financial status include death, ill health, critical illness, unemployment, etc. All these must be considered when purchasing a property through mortgage and adequate protection provision must be made for the family's peace of mind. Other possible financial liabilities are personal loans, credit cards, car loans, inheritance tax, etc. We will discuss how to address these risks later under protection products.

Age – Age is one of the major factors that dictates insurance premiums. The older you are, the more expensive your premium will be. It is for this reason that financial advisers always recommend that people take on insurance policy when they are still young as the premiums will be guaranteed throughout the policy term. Another advantage of taking out policy at very young age is the'clean health' status where there are no existing medical conditions which could be of concern for insurance providers and medical underwriters. The older you get, the greater the tendency that a health issue may arise, and even if none exists, insurance providers logically anticipate that something may go wrong, and so factor that into their premium assumptions. There are occasions whereby as a result of existing conditions, individuals become uninsurable or better still insured at rated premium.

Dependants – Financial dependency in the family comes in various forms. Primarily in the household, the husband has a measure of dependency on the wife and vice versa, even if either of them is not earning an income or supporting the family financially. There are some household responsibilities that the other partner will be dependent on the non-income earner for such as looking after the children, the house, and other domestic duties that the income earner cannot do due to his or her work schedule. Therefore, couples are deemed to have 'insurable interests' in each other. If there should be death or ill health of either of the two, there will be a void, and so, couples must pre-empt such void by putting an insurance in place for protection. In addition to their inter-dependence, they have protection responsibility towards their children to ensure that in any event of death of either or both of them, their children are catered for, able to complete their education and comfortable till they are financially independent. Apart from the children, there are occasions where the couple have people who may be adults and still dependant for many reasons like mental incapacitation or need for care. All these must be put into consideration when reviewing protection needs and objectives.

Existing Protection Provision – Some employers do make protection provision for their employees against death and ill health, making them unable to carry out their own occupation. Such provisions come in terms 'Death in Service' and 'Sickness pay'. Whatever provision is in existence must be taken into consideration.

Level of Income – The level of cover needed to protect income is subject to the level of that income and the amount of disposable income available to fund premium payment. The higher the income to be covered, the higher the premium required. Other factors that determine the premium outcome are deferred period, type of occupation and length of cover. We will elaborate further on these under insurance products.

Legacy – Many parents would like to leave a legacy of financial assets for their children. Passing estates to the next generation must be properly planned to ensure that what was supposed to be an asset doesn't become a liability. A very crucial aspect in passing legacy is Inheritance Tax planning. Within the United Kingdom, because there is a threshold of estate value after which inheritance tax sets in at 40%, parents must ensure their estates are planned and protected in such a way that they are passed to the next generation in a tax efficient way. Part of the strategy for estate planning is to put protection policy in place to cover any IHT liability within the estate so that the beneficiaries have sufficient funds to pay IHT liability when the settlors die.

PURPOSE OF LIFE INSURANCE POLICIES

The primary purpose of insurance can be summarised into two main headings: -

*Risk Transfer
*Wealth Transfer

Risk Transfer

Human beings generally are exposed to unpredictable risk in life. Such risk includes death, prolonged illness, critical illness, disability, accident and sickness, etc. All these unpredictable risks can have a negative impact on our financial plans and objectives, our families and the lives of people financially dependent on us. It is therefore wise to find a means of transferring this risk and providing protection for ourselves and our dependants. Apart from having more than enough cash to cater for such events, the alternative and preferred option is to put a life insurance policy in place to cover such risks.

History has it that the advent of life insurance dated back to 100 BC in Rome. A Roman military leader by the name of Caius Marius created a burial club among his troops so that when a member of the club died, the club would fund the funeral expenses out of their membership contributions and give money to the family of the deceased. This concept became attractive in Rome and grew with people joining burial clubs and making monthly contributions in hope that when they die, their families would benefit from the burial club membership intervention.

The reason why individuals gladly joined the clubs was to transfer the risk of burial and living expenses on the family from themselves to the burial clubs after members' death. The concept of insurance has since developed to what it is today, with opportunities to transfer unpredictable risk via insurance protection.

Through insurance contracts, individuals can now implement the following:

*Family Protection– Residence, Living Expenses and Children's education.

*Health & Income Protection– Critical Illness conditions, Accident, Sickness & Unemployment, Incapacitation and Disability.

Wealth Transfer

Effective transference of wealth from one generation to the other requires a great deal of financial planning. In advising and recommending suitable solutions to clients, implementing life insurance policies is a considerable option when it comes to Inheritance Tax planning. This ensures that estates are passed on to survivors in a tax-efficient way. Settlors of estates may have to put life insurance in place to ensure the beneficiaries have sufficient funds to pay IHT liability on the estate without any recourse to estate assets. Inheritance Tax payable on an individual estate when the owner dies is 40% of net estate after deductions of IHT Threshold which currently is £325,000.00. Net estate figure is the gross value of all assets including residence, cash, investment portfolios, etc owned by the individual less any liabilities.

For example, Mr. Popular whose net estate value is £1.2 million.

Net Estate Value	- £1,200,000.00
Less Threshold	- £325,000.00
	£875,000.00
IHT @ 40%	£350,000.00

The beneficiaries of Mr. Popular's estate must pay a sum of £350,000.00 before they can have access to the estate. The IHT liability has reduced the value of the estate from £1.2 million to £850,000.00 in the hand of the beneficiaries except he made a separate provision for how the IHT bill will be paid, by putting a life insurance in place in form of a Trust arrangement to ensure the sum assured sits outside of the estate, with his survivors as beneficiaries. More details about suitable life assurance products for such arrangements will be discussed under types of products.

TYPES OF LIFE INSURANCE PRODUCTS, USES AND FEATURES

There are different types of life insurance products designed by providers to serve different purposes. It is therefore important for individuals to seek advice before putting one in place. Due to my experience in the industry, I strongly recommend that individuals avoid the temptation of sourcing insurance via the internet or being sold to by salesmen who do not have a detailed information about the person's financial objectives and goals. The outcome of most of such actions is that people have insurance policies that do not meet their objectives. The most effective way of putting life insurance policy in place is to ensure that the policy is fit for purpose by giving consideration to the financial objectives and status of the client. I have met several clients who have one form of life insurance policy or the other quite alright, but it is not in alignment with their financial goals in any way. If they had to make a claim prior to meeting them, they would have been very disappointed. In this section l will discuss the different types of life insurance products and their usages.

-Term Assurance Policies

Term Assurance policies are designed to protect specific risks or liabilities for the period of time that the risk or liabilities exist only. After the stipulated time, the policy comes to an end and the life assured is no longer covered by the policy regardless of whether the risk still exists or not. The policy has no cash-in value, therefore, no return is given back to the life assured. The benefits of such policy is that if anything happens within the term of the policy, the policy will pay out the sum assured in line with the policy deed.

For example:

Mr. & Mrs. Potus recently bought their residential property with a mortgage borrowing of £200,000.00 on capital repayment basis with a term of 25 years. The purchase price was £300,000, which means they put a deposit (their own money) of £100,000.00 and their monthly mortgage repayment is £950.00. This property houses them and their two children who are 3 and 5 years of age respectively. They are both breadwinners for the family and jointly responsible for family running costs from their incomes.

Considering the above case study, there are different risks that Mr. & Mrs. Potus must consider and find a way of protecting themselves against. Firstly, the mortgage contract is for 25 years, probably the longest contract they will ever sign in their lifetime. Many things that are out of their control could happen such as:

*Ill Health
*Death
*Loss of Income
*Children's Education

These are unexpected events that can seriously affect the quality of living within the household. In addition to that, they have invested £100,000.00 of their own money into the purchase of the house, which must also be protected. Secondly, the property is the primary residence of the family and must be protected against any events that could disrupt their standard of living as highlighted above. It is the responsibility of Mr. & Mrs. Potus to seek advice to implement necessary plans to protect their financial arrangements and liabilities. The question then is, what options are available to them?

- **Mortgage Decreasing Term Assurance**

Mr. & Mrs. Potus should consider putting life insurance policies in place to cover the risks of death and critical illness. A suitable policy for this couple would be a Mortgage Decreasing Term Assurance because their mortgage arrangement is on capital repayment basis, which means the capital content of their mortgage decreases as the mortgage term of 25 years progresses. Therefore, they need life insurance policies that correlates with the mortgage arrangements. The initial sum assured for the policy would be £200,000.00, but this decreases as the policy term progresses, just as the capital content of the mortgage decreases. If within the mortgage term, a claim arises such as the death of or diagnosis of critical illness of either of the lives assured, the outstanding mortgage will be repaid by the policy subject to confirmation of accuracy of all information provided at the point of policy application. If there are any undisclosed health information relevant to application underwriting decision, providers may decline payment. It is for this reason that applicants are advised to ensure all relevant health conditions are declared in protection application form.

The life cover will reduce over the length of the policy. A certain interest rate will be used to calculate the life cover payable on death at any point in the future up to the end of the policy. The policy therefore will be only suitable for all loans with an average mortgage interest rate of up to and including the specified interest rate within the policy. It is advisable for individuals to ensure the rates within the policy is high enough to accommodate current mortgage rate and future hikes in rates. In most cases, the policy interest rates are always set far higher than mortgage rates.

Watch out for a statement similar to the following in your policy illustration:

The life cover will reduce over the length of the policy. An interest rate of 8 % is used to calculate the life cover payable on death at any point in the future up to the end of the policy. This policy is therefore only suitable for all loans with an average mortgage interest rate of up to and including 8 %.

- **Level Term Assurance**

Now, going back to Mr. & Mrs. Potus above, what if they had arranged their mortgage on Interest-Only basis, meaning the capital content of their mortgage borrowing remained the same throughout the mortgage term, unlike the above where the capital content was decreasing with the term? Since the capital borrowing would not decrease over the term, we need a corresponding policy with level sum assured throughout the 25 years term of the policy. Such policy is a Level Term Assurance, because the level of cover will remain the same throughout the policy term, the premium is usually higher in comparison with the Decreasing Term Assurance.

In both instances above, the policy ends after 25 years and Mr.& Mrs. Potus will no longer be covered regardless of whether they have finished paying off their mortgage or not. If either of them dies within the term of the policy, the policy provider will pay out a lump sum to the survivor or their estate depending on whether policy is structured on single or joint-life basis. Mostly, monthly premiums are always guaranteed. However, clients have a choice of reviewable premium in which case premium will be lower at the start of policy and will continue to increase throughout the policy term.

An important point to note is the benefits of integrating Critical Illness Cover into life insurance arrangements. Generally, critical illness cover is about five times more expensive than ordinary life cover because of the considered *value* of the benefits. Integrating a critical illness cover with ordinary life cover with £10.00 premium could change the premium to almost £60.00 or more. It is designed to cover serious health conditions such as cancer, heart disease, kidney disease, stroke etc. The definitions and conditions covered varies from provider to provider, therefore individuals putting life insurance in place with critical illness benefits must be informed about this.

> *Generally, critical illness cover is about five times more expensive than ordinary life cover because of the considered value of the benefits*

- **Family Income Benefit (FIB)**

Another consideration for Mr. & Mrs. Potus is the need for their monthly family expenses to be protected. As they are both breadwinners and have incomes supporting the family expenses, if something happens to either of them in terms of death or critical illness, the loss of income will definitely affect the household, except there is a provision in place. Their youngest child is 3 years old and financially dependent on them. Assuming the children would be supported up to age 21 when they finish their university education, Mr.& Mrs.

Potus need to think of how the monthly expenses will be met in addition to the cost of their children's education. The monthly expenses would be made up of mortgage payment, council tax, utility bills, travel, telephones/internet, loans, credit cards, higher purchase, food etc. Assuming the mortgage is paid off from the lump sum claim, other essential bills will still be outstanding of which the surviving partner may not be able to cater for. Therefore, they could arrange a Family Income Benefit with the total annual amount required of outstanding balance for household expenses as sum assured with a term till when the youngest child will reach the age of 21. Let us assume that the total household bill is £1,900.00 including mortgage. If the mortgage is paid off, the monthly bill reduces to £1,000.00 which means the family needs £12,000.00 annually for bill settlement for the next 18 years. Mr. & Mrs. Potus can put in place a Family Income Benefit policy with sum assured of £12,000.00 per annum with a term of 18 years.

In other words, FIB is a term assurance policy with a specified sum assured and paid annually to survivors or beneficiaries for a given period of term after which the policy comes to an end. Notice that the plan does not pay one-off lump sum as in Term Assurance policies above, but rather pays annually throughout the term of the policy if a claim arises. Because the policy doesn't pay lump sum up front, the premium is lower and cost-effective. Having made provision for living expenses, the couple need to think of the cost of education.

Establishing the cost of education involves three major commitments – Tuition, Accommodation and Pocket Money. The annual cost of this must be established and multiplied by the number of years of study to establish how much is required by each child to complete their university education. As the cost of education will not go down, a suitable policy for such arrangement will be a Level Term Assurance policy.

Notice that the plan doesn't not pay one-off lump sum as in Term Assurance policies above but rather pays annually throughout the term of the policy if a claim arises.)

- **Income Protection**

Income Protection policy is an income replacement insurance product that pays the life assured a predetermined level of benefit based on the individual's level of income in the event that such individuals are unable to carry out their occupation for a long term due to ill health. Most employers will have a sick pay policy in place, stipulating how long their employees will be paid if they are unable to work due to ill-health. After the stipulated period employers will stop the payment leaving the individual to cater for themselves. With an income replacement policy in place, individuals with prolonged ill-health can conveniently maintain their quality of life as the payments from such policy will be close to their net pay. In setting up the policy, the life assured has the options of level of payment, deferred period and definition of occupation qualified for payment. In the event of claim on income protection, the policy will continue to pay benefit until the person returns to work, retires or dies. Similar to this type of policy is Mortgage Payment Protection and Accident, Sickness and Unemployment policies. However, they differ in terms of level of cover and payment period in the event of a claim. We will discuss this under General Insurance.

- **Whole of Life Policies (WoL)**

Whole of Life policy is an insurance policy that covers the life assured throughout their entire life. The policy, unlike Term Assurance, is guaranteed to pay out at the death of life assured regardless of how long or short, as long as the owner pays the required premium till death occurs. Due to its features, WoL is used for transference of wealth from one generation to the other. In addition, this policy is widely used in estate planning, most especially in making provision for inheritance tax liabilities. The policy can be structured with cash-in value by building investment elements into it which means, if no claim is made, the policy builds in a cash-in value after a period of time– from around ten years. The owners can cash-in such policies if they are no longer of any use in their financial planning. However, standard whole of life policies are much more expensive in comparison with ordinary whole of life with maximum death benefit. The policy premium is guaranteed from inception for ten years after which premium will be reviewed.

In most cases, the premium goes up at review. Providers of Whole of Life policy will offer the following options at review: -

*New and higher premium for the same level of cover
*Same Premium for lower level of cover
*Higher premium for higher sum assured (if policy is indexed)

Whole of Life is generally suitable for family and estate protection. Policies can be written in single or joint names.

Whole of Life policy is an insurance policy that covers the life assured throughout their entire life. The policy unlike Term Assurance is guaranteed to pay out at the death of life assured regardless of how long or short, as long as the owner pays the required premium till the death event.)

GENERAL INSURANCE POLICIES

The term general insurance is a group name for insurance policies such as – Accident, Sickness & Unemployment policy, Private Medical Insurance, Mortgage Payment Protection, Buildings and Contents Insurance.

i. Accident, Sickness and Unemployment

This policy provides protection for individual against events such as accident, sickness and unemployment. A pre-determined amount of benefits will be agreed at inception of the policy for each event. Claims arises if the person is involved in an accident, takes ill and is unable to work or due to loss of employment. The agreed benefit will be paid for a period of between twelve to twenty-four months and then cease even if the person is still unable to work, unlike Income Protection that pays continuously till the person is back to work, dies or retires.

ii. Private Medical Insurance

This provides individuals the opportunity to access medical

treatment at a private level, choosing time, quality of care and preferred doctors. Many people are genuinely concerned about the waiting list for treatments by NHS. It is becoming popular for families and individuals to have private medical insurance in place either through workplace or via personal arrangements. Most providers are flexible with the level of benefits that are available, and clients can customise their medical treatment needs in some cases. Affordability is key word when it comes to private medical treatment. The more you can afford, the more you can get in terms of service.

iii. Mortgage Payment Protection

This is an insurance policy designated to protect the monthly mortgage if the owner is not able to pay due to accident, sickness or unemployment. The insurance policy will pay the monthly mortgage premium for a period of up to two years after which the payment stops and the individuals will have to continue. The difference between this type of cover and Income Protection includes limited payment period of maximum of two years and benefit payment in the event of unemployment. Also, the benefits usually cover the mortgage payment only. But with income protection, the life insured could have benefits very close to their normal monthly salary as the maximum policies pay up to is between 55-65% of gross income and is tax free.

From the general overview of life insurance features above, provision for such arrangements is an essential priority in individual financial planning and wealth creation objectives. Because most individuals may not have the required capital to cater for the liabilities and potential risks that can seriously impact the standard of living of themselves and their family, putting suitable life insurance policies in place to mitigate such unforeseen events must be attended to with utmost priority.

Chapter Action Points

***Purpose to put suitable life insurance provisions in place today to protect yourself and your family if you haven't done so before now.**

***Seek professional advice to review an existing plan, most especially if you've had the policies for many years without any review.**

***Ensure your policies are put in Trusts where necessary for IHT purposes and to guarantee that benefits are rightly allocated to your nominated beneficiaries.**

***Ensure you have the right policies for right purposes with the right sum assured to cater for any liability within your estate.**

***Couples must ensure their spouse is equally protected. Even though liability may be on single name basis, insurable interest exists for couples.**

SAVINGS & INVESTMENTS

SAVINGS & INVESTMENTS

The Savings and Investments sector of UK financial system is dynamic and is designed in such a manner that it caters for all interested investors young or old regardless of level of income. All interested investors will find something suitable for their objectives. It is important that we distinguish between savings and investments as they are often misconstrued.

Savings

Savings are designed for keeping money for a near time prime purpose. In other words, the money is kept away but needed soon and therefore must be accessible when needed. The priority here therefore is liquidity, accessibility without any exposure to volatility and risk of loss. Therefore, capital security is important as fund is needed on short term. As the fund is not exposed to risk, returns on savings are usually minimal. Due to all of the above savings are therefore in forms of cash or bonds assets which will offer a certain percentage of returns upfront as reward for investors i.e., they know what level of returns they will get as they put their money into savings schemes. Savings is therefore suitable for short term objectives, which are objectives under five years, and for emergency funds. It is not wise to use savings for medium to long term objectives because of its limited or lack of growth. The funds are cash based and savings scheme are vulnerable to inflation. In real terms, inflation may erode the value of money, if rate of inflation is greater than that of returns on savings. Therefore any fund that is not needed on short term must be invested to add value through growth opportunities.

Savings is therefore suitable for short term objectives, which are objectives under five years, and for emergency funds. It is not wise to use savings for medium to long term objectives because of its limited or lack of growth.

Investments

Investments are suitable for clients that are looking for opportunities to grow their money on medium to long term basis. The whole objective of investments is to take advantage of market movements by investing in different asset classes to maximise returns. Investors funds are therefore invested in different asset classes at various proportions which is in line with clients objectives, investment time horizon, level of investment, investment experience, attitude to risk and capacity for loss. These should be captured by the financial adviser at the initial meeting. The investment market is regulated in the UK; therefore most investments will require meeting a qualified and authorised individuals licensed to give financial advice. With investments there is no foreknowledge of what the returns will be. However, there will be evidence of past performance which is never an indication of future returns. No one can predict future performance. Investment provides opportunities to invest in equity-based collectives which are pools of investments to achieve growth. Generally investing in equity-based portfolio over medium to long term basis have proven time and time over to be good value to investors, as it has out-performed other asset classes several times.

Investment provides opportunities to invest in equity-based collectives which are pools of investments to achieve growth.

Risk & Reward

For all investors, understanding the balance between risk and reward is the key to the success of their investment experience. Generally, all investments involve a measure of risk. Investors therefore must be prepared to take a measure of risk to achieve their medium to long term financial goals.

To develop a suitable investment strategy for investors, in addition to understanding investment objectives and capacity for loss, it is important to understand their readiness to take risk which may result in losses, for thc gains they are looking for. It is impossible to eliminate risk when investing, however a proper assessment by advisers and good understanding by investors helps to manage the risk by ensuring a suitable investment portfolio is constructed to meet the individual's investment objectives. Basic principles that must be considered by both advisers and investors includes the following – ensure the individual have enough cash to meet emergency and short-term needs, time frame of investments, the effects of inflation on investment, diversifying investments across different asset classes to reduce risk within the minimal risk appetite to adventurous with a high level of risk appetite. Investors with a cautious risk profile outcome will have a higher percentage of cash and bonds in their investment portfolio while investors with adventurous risk profile will have minimal cash and bonds with large proportions of portfolio invested in equities. Going through the risk profiling exercise with investors will help determine their attitude to risk and capacity for loss.

When investing, the following risks are possibilities: -

*Your investment could reduce in value – most especially at the early days of your investments, due to deduction of investment charges, your investment value may be lower than what you put in.

*Your investment may be negatively impacted by inflation. This applies to cautious investor where portfolio carries minimal risk and therefore minimal potential for returns. Though the investment figure may be there but over longer-term low returns on investments will erode value of funds due to inflation.

*You may not be able to afford a fall in value. Individuals that solely rely on income from their investment's portfolio might be vulnerable in a down market as the level of income will drop which may affect their standard of living.

*You may not be able to access your fund when you need it. Some investments are not easily sellable. In addition, to avoid loss, investors will avoid accessing their portfolio in a down market.

ASSET CLASSES

In the investment world, there are four major asset classes. These are Cash, Bonds, Equities and Property. The fifth category called Alternative Investments consists of assets that do not fall into any of the major four categories stated above.

Cash – All savings in Banks and Building Societies including fixed deposits fall into this category. The money market also belongs to this group of asset class. Although the value of fund is protected, interest rates could fall and cash assets may not be able to keep up with inflation.

Bonds – Are ways through which government of nations and corporate organisation borrows money from investors. They offer investors a fixed return of interest on their investments. The full capital amount invested is returned at the end of the investment with varying terms. Although bonds are viewed to have a measure of security however, they are less secured in comparison with cash. They are also sensitive to interest rates and inflation movements. An increase in interest or inflation rates will result in a fall in bond value. The capital value of the bonds are linked with the financial strength and stability of the borrower. It is generally believed that the government bonds are more financially strong and stable in comparison with corporate bonds. The reason being that it is easier for corporate organisations to go bankrupt when compared with the government. For this reason, the rate of returns on corporate bonds are generally higher than that of government bonds. Other factor that causes sensitivities to bond market is the term to maturity. Bonds with shorter terms are less sensitive in comparison with bonds with longer terms. Corporate bonds come in different grades. High yield bonds carries higher risk while investment grades bonds are more secured as they are issued by companies with good financial strength.

Equities – Is a way of owning companies by individuals and companies by buying their shares for investment purposes. The value of shares is connected with the company's success and profitability. Company shares are more volatile in comparison to bonds and cash and produce greater returns over medium to long term. As shares value are sensitive to market movements, investors must note that the value goes up and down and some shares are far more volatile than others. In developed countries, company shares are less of a risk in comparison with underdeveloped or developing nations where the risk is higher. Such markets are referred to as emerging markets. Emerging markets comes with a greater potential for returns due to the high risk nature of their shares.

Property – Is an indirect way of investing into property. Through property funds, investors invest into a diversified portfolio of commercial property funds. People with smaller funds have the opportunity of pooling resources together via property fund managers investing in commercial properties. Although the value of investments in property portfolio also fluctuates but not as volatile as equities. Advantages of investing in commercial property portfolio includes the ability to generate income for investors looking for income. However, it should be noted that investment is illiquid as commercial properties may take a long time to sell when investors want to have their capital back. Investors with small capital but desiring to invest in property can take advantage of investing in commercial property funds. Through such collective investment, they benefit from income and possibly capital gains if they remain invested in portfolio by the time the property is sold. In addition, they benefit from professional management and are freed totally from unpredictable landlords' roles and responsibilities.

Alternative Investments – Are assets that do not fall into main assets classes. Such assets includes commodities such as line oil, gold, timber, cocoa, tin, ore etc. As part of strategy for diversification, some investors will include some of these assets in their portfolio. Such assets may be accessed through "Derivatives", which means they are derived from products. A Derivative is a contract. The contract trades through a platform otherwise called Exchange. The contract is an agreement to make payment or otherwise deliver some goods (underlying goods) on the outcome of certain future event, at a pre-agreed date and price. The contracts can be issued by financial institutions including investment banks and the contract value changes in line with market movements of the underlying assets whether its equities, bonds, currencies, or commodities. Fund managers, as part of risk diversification strategy have exposure to alternative assets via derivatives. The aim is to reduce volatility of returns, investing in such assets comes with potential risk of failure by financial institutions that issued the contract to fulfil their obligations.

PRINCIPLES OF SAVINGS & INVESTMENTS

For individuals to build investment portfolio, there are underlying factors that must be considered. These factors are essential for successful investment experience. Applying the principles makes the journey easier and achievable. In an attempt to create wealth, considerations must be given to the following: -

Investment Objectives – This is answering "why" an individual wants to put the investment in place. To avoid frivolous attitude towards their portfolios, individuals must be very clear about their reason for putting the investments in place. It must be something very dear and of great value.

To build a successful investment portfolio there must be a compelling reason that an individual considers to be rewarding both now and in the future. Such reasons could be buying first property, building capital to fund retirement income, building capital to fund desired lifestyle, funds for children education, first car, first property, capital to fund business growth or a new start-up etc. The objective keeps investor focused.

Time Frame – Potential investors must be very clear in their mind the time frame for their investments. Generally, the time frame will fall into three categories – Short, Medium and Long term. Short term is anything less than five years, while medium term is between 5 – 15 years and Long term is any investment more than 15 years.

This is very important as it determines the type of investments and assets that would be suitable for investor's objectives. For instance, if an individual is keeping funds away for deposit for property purchase in two to three year's time, this would be considered as a short term investment. Clients will prefer not to expose such funds to a volatile asset but rather to stable assets such as cash and bonds.

Investing therefore for a short-term objective should be in a less volatile safe asset, where there's a measure of guarantee that the investor will not lose money, such as cash-based asset and bonds. However, investors must understand that returns on such assets are very minimal. In addition, the prevailing rate of inflation must be taken into consideration. Should the rate of inflation be higher than the interest rate on investment, it means the value of invested capital will be eroded by higher inflation. It is therefore advisable that investors keep emergency funds only in cash. Any capital for medium to longer term objectives must be invested.

Medium to long term investment provides individuals the opportunity to grow their capital over a period of time. Investors looking for growth opportunities and to beat inflation could invest in a more diversified portfolios consisting of not just cash or bonds but also equities, properties, and alternative investments. This reduces the risk in portfolio as it provides opportunities for the portfolio to reflect the risk profile of investors. It also helps to profit from market movements as the companies they invest in make profit. However, in contrast with such exposure, investors could lose money in low markets. The benefit of investing for a medium to long time is that there is enough time to stay in the market to recoup any loss. The caveat therefore is that investors must be well equipped and prepared to ride out low market by staying in the market during such period with professional advice and support from their financial adviser.

Most investment plans towards retirement will fall into long term.

Medium to long term investment provides individuals the opportunity to grow their capital over a period of time.

Target

This could be to pay off the outstanding balance of mortgage borrowing on a residential property for a particular period e.g. in 10 years time. Such a target creates a form of something to look forward to and brings fulfilment when the target is met. The target helps strengthen the reason for the investment portfolio and the purpose for whatever sacrifice the individual is making to build the investment portfolio. With the purpose in mind, investors are more likely to stay invested regardless of financial challenges, except when it is unavoidably necessary for them to disinvest.

Discipline

Without discipline most investment plans and objectives will not be achieved. Many derailed their investment plans due to lack of discipline. I've come across many stories, reasons and excuses that connotes nothing but financial indiscipline. People disinvest their financial portfolio to spend the money on things that have nothing to do with their financial goals and objectives. To create wealth for your future you may have to deny yourself of certain pleasures now. If you lack financial discipline, your financial goals and aspirations will remain nothing but mere wishes. Individuals that create wealth are people who subject themselves to self-discipline to achieve their financial dreams.

If you lack financial discipline, your financial goals and aspirations will remain nothing but mere wishes.)

Risk & Reward Principle

In the world of investment, risk and reward goes hand in hand. All investments have one form of risk or the other. Therefore the four major asset classes can be affected by one form of risk or the other. Common risks within an investment portfolio are inflation risk, interest rate risk, volatility risk, liquidity, counter-party risk, exchange rate risk, political risk, market risk, non-systemic risk, organisational risk, legislative risk, and many more. Investors should realise that it is impossible to invest without taking a measure of risk even if you invest in cash. You are exposed to inflation risk, if inflation rate is higher than your savings rate, then inflation could erode the value of your money. You are also exposed to interest rate risk, interest rate may fall therefore you get less return on your savings. Another risk is the institution keeping your money may run into financial difficulties and may not be able refund all your money back to you. Since we cannot eliminate risk completely from investment portfolio, the strategy is to manage risk by investment managers. Managing risks within client's portfolio entails understanding client's investment objectives, attitude to risk, capacity for loss, diversifying portfolio and investment time frame. With a proper understanding of these factors investment advisers can establish client overall risk profile and a proper portfolio can be constructed that will provide a balance between risk taken and expected reward. The portfolio will be made up of all different asset classes in different proportions relevant to the risk profile.

Usually, investment risk spectrum runs from Low to Adventurous. An example of risk spectrum is shown below. An individual with a low risk profile will likely have more of cash and bonds and less equities in comparison with an adventurous individual. The higher the risk, the greater the potentials for higher returns. Investors looking for higher returns therefore must be willing to take higher risk. Higher risk simply means exposure to more volatile asset classes such as equities of large and small companies in different parts of the world including emerging markets.

> *Investors should realise that it is impossible to invest without taking a measure of risk even if you invest in cash*

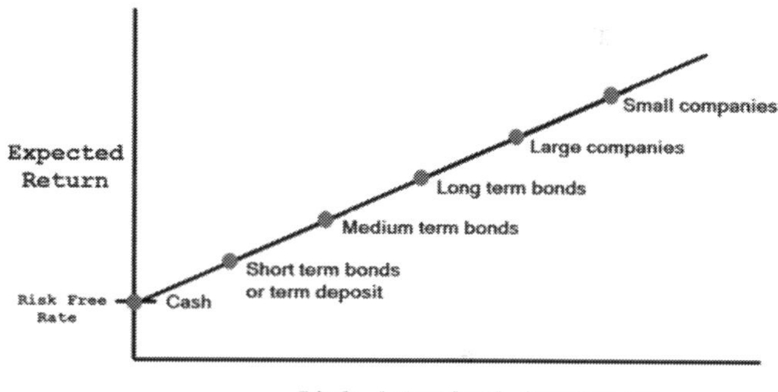

LOW → LOWER-MEDIUM → MEDIUM → UPPER-MEDIUM → HIGH

Fig 4 – *Risk Spectrum*

Investment Products in the United Kingdom

There are various investment products in the United Kingdom financial services industry making it possible for all intending investors to invest, regardless of age or the level of resources available. There's something for everyone resident in the United Kingdom to take advantage of to achieve their investment plans and objectives. Investment products available include but not limited to the following:-

*Friendly Savings Society
*National Savings & Investments products
*Investment Bonds
*Individual Savings Accounts
*OEIC's & Unit Truts
*Investment Trusts
*Venture Capital Trusts (VCT)
*Enterprise Investments Scheme (EIS)
*Seed Enterprise Investment Scheme (SEIS)
*Hedge Funds & Derivatives
*Commodities.

Chapter Action Points

***Purpose to start an investment portfolio today either via lump sum or regular contributions.**

***Available funds for future financial objectives on medium to long term should be invested for growth opportunity.**

***Emergency and short-term objective should remain in cash.**

***Seek professional advice to review any existing investment portfolio to ensure satisfactory performance.**

***Maximise all tax-efficient investments allowances with available resources.**

***Have a target in mind and focus on your target. Avoid distraction.**

***Be disciplined.**

PENSIONS

PENSIONS

Investing towards old age is an important aspect of financial planning in the United Kingdom. Building up capital to fund income at retirement must be prioritise in individuals financial planning goals and objectives because at retirement, income from employment ceases and sustenance now depends on what individuals have put away during their earning days either through their employers' schemes or their own personal arrangements. Research have shown that people are living longer due to medical advancement, which means people will need more money to survive during their retirement years. Generally, to build up substantial amount of capital for retirement income may take up to forty years. It is advisable that people commence contributing into pensions, as early as they can.

In the United Kingdom, there are three possible ways an individual can build up pensions for their retirement. These are – State Pension, Occupational Pension and Personal Pension arrangements. Let us examine each of these options and their features.

In the United Kingdom, there are three possible ways an individual can build up pensions for their retirement. These are – State Pension, Occupational Pension and Personal Pension arrangements

State Pension

Individuals during their working life in the United Kingdom make National Insurance (NI) contributions in additions to tax deductions. Both payments are deducted via Pay As You Earn (PAYE) system from their wages and the net pay is their final take home. The amount of National Insurance deductions is based on individuals' level of earnings. The NI contributions is mandatory if you are 16 years of age or over and employed or self-employed and making profit of £6,515 or more a year.

Class 1 – For employees earning more than £184 per week and under State Pension age.

Class 2 – Self-Employed people earning profits of £6,515 or more per year.

Class 3 – Voluntary NI contributions to fill any NI gap or to avoid any gap in payment record.

Class 4 – Self-employed earning profits of £9,569 or more a year.

In addition to the above, it is worth mentioning that companies do make NI contributions on their employee's benefits and expenses. Companies' contributions are classified as Class 1A or 1B. Class 1A NIC is applicable on expenses and benefits while Class 1B contributions is applicable for anything else. The rate for Class 1 NIC contribution for 2021/22 is 12% of earning between £797 to £4,189 per month and 2% over £4,189 a month.

The National insurance contribution is essential for individual to qualify for certain benefits and state pensions. Such benefits include contribution-based job seeker allowance, contribution-based Employment and Support Allowance, Maternity Allowance and Bereavement Support Payment.

Your national insurance contributions determines the amount of State Pension benefit when an individual comes to state retirement age. The more contributions you have made over the years the more your state pension up to the maximum amount. The maximum amount of new state pension for 2021/22 is £179.60 per week. You can earn above this figure only if you have additional state pension benefits or deferred your pension benefits. Government adjusts the figure annually to reflect inflation. To earn state pension an individual must have worked and made National Insurance contributions for ten qualifying years. The ten years do not have to be in a row but aggregate of NIC's contributions during your working years. Please note that the ten years is minimal qualifying years for you to qualify for any state pension.

At state retirement age, your state pension entitlement will be calculated by firstly determining your "starting amount" based on your contributions record before 2016. Your "starting amount" will be the higher of:-

- ·*The amount you will get under the old State Pension rules
- ·*The amount you will get if the new pension had been in place at the beginning of your working life.

You can add more qualifying years to your State Pension to increase your pension benefits if your starting amount is below full state pension benefits by making voluntary contributions. In any event if your starting amount is more than full new state pension, then the portion over is called "protected payment" which will be paid on top of your state pension.

If for any reason you have no NIC's record before 2016 then your state pension benefits will be calculated under the new State Pension rules. Please note that although you need ten years to be qualified for any State Pension, you actually need thirty-five working years to be qualified for full state pension. You can always request for your state pension forecast from https://www.gov.uk/check-state-pension and other useful information are available from the website.

From the above, the State Pension on its own may not be enough for many and therefore additional provision may be required to have sufficient capital to fund income at retirement. At retirement, individual's quality of life could go up or down or remain the same. Any of these outcomes are a factor of how much has been built up by individuals over the years to fund income at retirement. It is more advantageous for people to commence contributions into pensions early.

To earn state pension an individual must have worked and made National Insurance contributions for ten qualifying years. The ten years do not have to be in a row but aggregate of NIC's contributions during your working years.

Occupational Pensions

Otherwise referred to as workplace pensions, it forms part of the benefits that employers of labour put in place for their employees. Organisation used this as an incentive to demonstrate to their workforce that they are interested in their future and willing to invest in it. Some organisations use this as part of their strategy to attract experienced employees to their company. The company normally sets up the scheme and make contributions on behalf of their employees into the scheme. Their contribution is usually a certain percentage of employee's remuneration. These contributions are in addition to employee's salaries therefore it is an additional benefit to the employee. The scheme may be designed to be – Contributory or Non-Contributory. Contributory mandates the employee to contribute into the scheme while Non-Contributory scheme is not mandatory. The employer will continue to contribute even if the employee does not make any contribution. The workplace scheme could be either a Final Salary or Money Purchase scheme.

These contributions are in addition to employee's salaries therefore it is an additional benefit to the employee.)

Final Salary (Defined Benefit - DB)

A final salary scheme also known as Defined Benefit (DB) scheme is the type of scheme where the employee's benefit is calculated based on last salary and the number of years in service as a proportion of the scheme year. For example, if an employee works with an organisation with a final salary scheme for a period of 20 years and his salary before he left the organisation was £30,000 per annum, and the scheme retirement year is 60. The entitlement of that individual will be calculated as 20/60 x £30,000. His pension benefit from that scheme will be £10,000 per annum. Some schemes do have additional lump sum benefits built into employee's benefits. For example, let's assume the scheme above has additional lump sum benefits of 3/80th, the lumpsum payment from the scheme will be calculated as 3/80 x £30,000 x 20 years, giving the employee a lump sum pay out of £22,5000. Contributions are made into the scheme during working years of the employee by both employee and the employer. Employee's contributions are always a certain percentage of salary which is deducted from gross salary before tax. This makes pension contributions via employers' scheme to be tax-efficient as the contributions enjoy tax relief. Other features that may be available with final salary schemes are dependants, spouse, and death-in-service benefits. This varies from one scheme to the other in line with the scheme rules and regulation. It is important that scheme members familiarise themselves with the scheme rules and regulations.

At retirement the individual has a choice of taking the pension benefits from the scheme or transfer the benefits from the scheme to a more flexible scheme with various options of taking pension income if the person is looking for flexibilities with pension income drawdown. An important caveat here is that, due to regulatory framework within the industry, the person must seek independent professional advice for pension transfer from qualified and authorised financial adviser. This requires that the adviser request the Statement of Entitlements from the scheme administrators.

The cash equivalent transfer value of employee's benefit will be documented in the statement. The adviser will conduct various analysis including critical yield calculation to make any transfer recommendation. Final recommendation depends on the outcome of analysis whether the employee will be better off or disadvantaged with the transfer. The recommendation must be fully justified before transfer would be allowed. The suitability for transfer takes into consideration client's situations and circumstances including financial objectives and goals, and other assets available to fund retirement income.

An important caveat here is that, due to regulatory framework within the industry, the person must seek independent professional advice for pension transfer from qualified and authorised financial adviser.)

As financial situations and objectives differ from individual to individual, pension transfer will be suitable for some people and not others. For example, an individual that wants guaranteed income and has no other assets to fund retirement income, a transfer would not be advisable while for an individual who has other sources of income and other assets and is not particular about guaranteed income, then transfer could be suitable subject to considering all other factors and features of the scheme. Another important factor about DB scheme is statutory increase which increases members benefit automatically to reflect the impact of inflation on annual basis. Such benefits are of great importance when considering benefits transfer, because of its value in increasing member's benefits continually in line with inflation.

Transferring pension from defined benefit scheme – UFPLUS or FAD

When occupational pension benefits are transferred from the scheme, to benefit from flexibilities in drawing down pension income, they are transferred into Uncrystallised Funds Pension Lump Sum (UFPLS) or Flexible Access Drawdown pots, depending on the objcctives, needs and circumstances of the individual. The difference between both options is in drawing down of tax-free lump sums. With FAD, the tax-free lump sum is drawn once, and the rest of the fund is taxable while with UFPLS, 25% of every amount drawn from the pot is tax free while the remaining 75% is taxable. More details about this will be made available in the Pension Handbook by same author.

Defined Contributions (DC, Money Purchase or Personal Pension)

Apart from some companies with existing DB Schemes, most companies have opted for Money Purchase schemes instead of Defined Benefits schemes. The main reason is that DB is costlier for organisations in comparison with DC schemes due to the statutory increases engraved into such schemes. With DC schemes, members are only entitled to the value of their investment at retirement without any statutory increase obligation from their employer.

The Defined Contribution scheme is normally structured as an investment-based schemes. The contributions from both employers and employees are invested and managed by investment managers appointed by the scheme Trustees for growth purposes. The investment company will set up a group pension otherwise called Group Pension Plan (GPP) and qualified employees of the company will be registered members of the schemes. A certain percentage of qualified member's income will be deducted as their contributions to the scheme and employers will contribute certain percentage into the scheme also. Whatever is contributed by both parties are invested and managed by the investment company till the scheme's retirement age when members can draw down from their pension. In any event that the member leaves the company before retirement age, they have the option of leaving the pension with the provider or they can move their pension with them to a new employer's scheme if permitted to do so or to an independent financial advisory firm for management. This is possible because within the group scheme, every employee has their independent pots with unique policy number.

The pension provider usually invests the pension funds in different asset classes in line with the risk profile of members looking for growth opportunities. The fund managers have the daily management oversight responsibilities of the funds. The performance of the funds will determine the growth within member's portfolios. Other factors that affect returns are charges applicable within the portfolios.

Personal Pension Plans

Personal pension are pension arrangements put in place by individuals to fund their income at retirement. In the United Kingdom, putting a personal pension plan in place requires individuals employing the services of qualified and authorised financial advisers because pension investment is a regulated product. The regulatory framework requires that the adviser conduct a Fact Find exercise otherwise known as Know Your Client. This exercise entails taking information about the client's retirement plan objectives, risk profile, other assets available and other relevant soft information. With this information, advisers could conduct a research and construct an investment portfolio suitable to meet client's retirement objectives. Through this exercise, the individual can begin to make contributions into their pension pot through regular or lump sum contributions or combinations of both, to be managed by fund managers till the selected retirement age. This phase of building up pension is called the "accumulative phase" of pension contribution.

Contribution from individuals enjoys tax relief based on person's marginal rate of tax i.e basic, higher or additional higher rate of tax. Generally, all contributions get the basic rate tax relief at source. Higher rate and additional rate taxpayers have to make further claims through their self-assessment returns. For example, a person contributing £500 (net) per month into his pension will receive a relief of £125from the government to make his invested fund a total of £625.A higher rate taxpayer can make a further claim of £125 via self-assessment return while an additional rate taxpayer £156.25 through same system.

Individuals with Personal Pension pot also can invest lump sum amount to their pension scheme subject to a maximum amount of annual allowance which is currently £40,000 for 2021/22 financial year. Although individuals can invest more than the annual allowance, but tax relief will only be available on the annual allowance. Also, all individuals can invest £3,600 per annum or maximum amount of their annual pensionable income. Therefore, while all individuals can invest as much as £3,600 including children, someone with an income of £50,000 can invest as much as £50,000 into his pension pot with full tax relief on £40,000 only except the person have unused allowance that can be carry forward to current financial year. Contributions can take the form of regular contributions or lump sum contributions or combinations of both. It's always advisable that people use up their allowable allowance subject to available resources.

For example, a person contributing £500 (net) per month into his pension will receive a relief of £125 from the government to make his invested fund a total of £625. A higher rate taxpayer can make a further claim of £125 via self-assessment return while an additional rate taxpayer £156.25 through same system.

Self-Invested Pension Plan – (SIPP)

Is a type of personal pension plan for individuals who desires more than the generic personal pension investment strategy and will like to be involved in the investment decisions of his or her pension portfolio. Certain individuals will like to involve assets such as stocks and shares of single companies, commercial properties, arts in their pension investment portfolio. SIPP is designed to accommodate such individual's pension investment objectives. Due to its structure and non-generic investment strategy, SIPP charges are usually higher than a conventional pension plan.

The attractions to SIPP are the features such as the ability to control investments and wide investment choices. However, SIPP is not for everyone, except for people who really have the desire to make their own investment decisions with confidence and knowledge to do so. With SIPP, although individuals may be involved in investment decision, but the daily management of the pension portfolio is the responsibility of the fund managers.

Small Self Administered Scheme – SSAS

This is a form of pension scheme put in place and managed by the employer for the benefits of senior staff and directors of a small company or family business. SASS schemes do not require the intervention of financial or insurance institutions but purely managed by the scheme administrator and Trustees of the scheme who may be a member of the scheme. Usually scheme memberships are not more than twelve and this could be company directors, their relatives and other senior management employees of the company. Apart from the freedom of choosing how the pension funds are invested, SSAS schemes has the additional benefit of investing scheme funds in their company. A company is permitted to operate only one SSAS scheme. Like SIPP, the scheme can invest in diverse asset classes including commercial properties. Other attractive features of SSAS is the ability of the scheme to offer commercial loans to the company to purchase asset such as commercial property for business operations. Rental incomes from the commercial property are then put back into the pension fund. SSAS are also allowed to borrow money via a mortgage transaction for investment purposes. Contributions made into SSAS enjoys tax reliefs as explained above in line with member's marginal rate of tax.

Pension Tax Efficiency

One of the most attractive features of contributing into a pension scheme is the tax-efficiency of the scheme via tax-reliefs. Both the contributions and the pension portfolio enjoy one form of tax advantage or the other. Contributions from all sources are grossed up in value. Employee's contributions are deducted from their salaries before tax which means the amount of funds going into the pension scheme is tax-free. This arrangement is referred to as "net pay". Also, employer's contributions are not taxed either, adding value to members' pension.

On the other hand, contributions into individual pension's plans enjoys tax-relief through "relief at source" arrangement. In this case, all contributions from individuals into the scheme have immediate increase by basic rate tax relief which is 20% of gross contributions. Therefore, an individual with a desire to put £500 into his pension plan only contribute £400 and the government will add £100 to make up the £500. Higher rate and additional higher rate taxpayers will have to claim further reliefs through their self-assessment returns in line with their marginal rate of tax. A higher rate taxpayer may claim further relief of 20% while an additional rate taxpayer may claim 25% further tax reliefs. It's this feature in pension contributions that makes it beneficial and advisable for higher rate and additional rate taxpayers to maximise contributions into pensions as it reduces drastically tax liabilities on their income. Parts of their income that would have gone to the tax man are directed towards their pension pots instead.

Pension fund's portfolio also enjoys great tax advantage. The investment portfolios are free of income and capital gain tax giving such funds huge advantages over other funds with such liabilities.

Therefore, an individual with a desire to put £500 into his pension plan only contribute £400 and the government will add £100 to make up the £500.

Pension via Limited Liability Companies

Making contributions via Limited Liability companies could be of great value to company directors for tax purposes. For directors of a limited liability company, the company can fund pension contributions from company revenues. Such contributions are considered as *business expense* for tax purposes. However, the money is not spent but rather invested into the director's pension pot for the benefit of individual directors or senior personnel of the organisation.

Such contributions could reduce the amount of taxable profit thereby reducing the amount of tax liability for the company. For example, assume Company A made a profit of £40,000 and the director decided to put the whole £40,000, which is the maximum allowance for this financial year into pension investment for his own benefit, the tax liability for that financial year will be zero avoiding a corporation tax of 19%. Contributions via a limited liability company is a good way to extract profit from company account to mitigate tax liability and increase investment opportunity.

Contributions via a limited liability company is a good way to extract profit from company account to mitigate tax liability and increase investment opportunity.

Stakeholder Pension Schemes

Over the years the pension regimes have experienced changes as a result of the government trying to encourage citizens to contribute into pension schemes. Stakeholder pension is one of such efforts by the government to make pension easily accessible by all. The scheme was designed to make provisions for middle- and low-income earners who have no privilege of joining employer's occupational scheme such that individuals can set up their own scheme.

Employers without any scheme in place have to offer a stakeholder scheme for their employees. The scheme was designed to be portable; employees can move with their pension pot when they leave their employer. It is flexible and low cost in management with annual management charges capped at maximum 1% and minimum contributions set at £20 regular or lump sum. Despite the low cost and simplistic nature of the scheme, it has all the features of a personal pension schemes.

Individuals can contribute £3,600 a year or 100 % of earnings up to maximum annual allowance which is currently £40,000 with tax relief. Stakeholder can be set up for children and working individuals. Contributions from third parties are also allowed such as spouses contributions on behalf of their partners, grandparents for grandchildren etc. Owners of Stakeholder pensions can access their pension scheme from the age of 55 with 25% as tax free cash lump sum and the rest of the fund is taxable at their marginal rate of tax.

Pension Simplifications – "A-Day"

Prior to 6th April 2006, otherwise refereed as the A-Day within UK pension industry, different pension schemes have different rules and regulations with regards to tax applicable. The main objective of A Day was to unify the taxation of pension for uniformity in the United Kingdom. With effect from the day, individuals are allowed to invest as much as !00% of their earnings into any number of pension schemes however with some caveat. Tax relief on contributions is subject to two important factors: -

* Annual Allowance – Individuals contributions must not exceed the annual allowance otherwise; the excess attracts a tax liability of 40%.

* Lifetime Allowance – When individuals are ready to take their benefits at their selected retirement age or reaches the age of 75, their entire pension values will be tested against the lifetime allowance which was originally set at £1.5 million at A-Day. The figures have changed over the years and the applicable lifetime allowance to individuals will be the figure at the year of retirement. If pension value exceeds the lifetime allowance at retirement, the excess will attract a tax of 25% if taken as pension income or 45% if taken as a lump sum.

To prevent individuals who have saved more than lifetime allowance being at a disadvantaged, two types of protection were introduced to protect their benefits. These are – (i) Primary Protection and (ii) Enhanced Protection.

<u>The Primary Protection</u> - values individual's pension pot as at 6th April 2006 and will give an uplift relative to the life time allowance. For example, if Mr A pension value as at A-Day was£2.0 million which was £500,000 or 25% greater than the lifetime allowance, Mr A will have a lifetime allowance of 1.25 times when he comes to retirement which would be

25% more than the £1.5 million protected from any recovery charge.

Enhanced Protection – protects member's benefits from any recovery charge regardless of the value, however members ought to have ceased contributions into the scheme prior to 6th April 2006.

Also prior to A-Day, different schemes have different rules with regards to lump sum pay. From A-Day, all schemes can pay a tax-free lump sum of 25% of member's pension value and the rest will be taxed according to individual tax rate. If the existing scheme rules allows more than 25%, members can apply for protection to protect their tax-free cash lump sum value also.

Auto-Enrolment

This is a government initiative introduced in 2012 as part of their efforts to encourage pension contributions by employers and employees. All organisations with a minimum of one eligible employee must automatically enrol the employee in a pension scheme. All employers must contribute into the pension plan for their eligible employees. From 2012 the scheme was phased out starting with larger companies first till 2018 when all companies must have duly put in place a scheme for the benefits of their employees. The motive behind the drive by the government is from their observation that many people are not saving for retirement and this could put a burden on the government in the future.

The government envisage that the State Pension may not be sufficient for many, plus government resources may be limited because people are living longer. To encourage workers to build up savings for retirement, the government introduced a reform through Pension Act 2008 compelling all employers to set up a scheme and automatically enrol all eligible workers.

Setting up a scheme requires the employer to categorise the workforce into the following three categories:

Eligible Jobholders - will be automatically enrolled. To be an eligible worker, you must be aged 22 and State Pension age, with earnings above the threshold of £10,000, and work or ordinarily work in the UK and you have a contract of employment. Workers within this category must be automatically enrolled by their employers without any actions from them.

Non-Eligible - are workers within the age bracket of 16 and 21, or age between State Pension age and 74 with earnings over the threshold, and work or ordinarily work in the UK with contract of employment or individuals who are aged between 16 and 74 and have earnings between lower earnings amount and the earnings threshold of £10,000 and work or ordinarily work in the UK and have a contract of employment in place. Workers within this category are not automatically enrolled but have the rights to ask to join the scheme. If they do ask, the employer must enrol them and contribute to the scheme on their behalf.

Entitled Worker - are workers within the age bracket of 16 to 74, with earning below the lower earnings amount and work or ordinarily work in the UK with employment contract. They have the right to ask to join the scheme, however employers have no obligation to contribute into the scheme although they may choose to do so.

Opt-Out Option

Eligible Jobholders can opt out if they do not want to be part of the scheme. If they exercise the Opt-Out option within the first month of their enrolment, their contribution will be returned back to them in full, however only their contributions will be return not the employers' contributions nor the tax relief. Employee must complete the opt-out form and send to scheme provider to exercise their right. If you decide to opt-out after a month, no refund will be made but rather contributions will remain in the pot until you can access pension benefits. The earliest age now to access pension benefits is 55. The Opt-Out option last for three years after which the employer must automatically re-enrol eligible jobholders. This must be repeated after every three years. Eligible Jobholders can also choose to opt-out or not at this point. The reason for this exercise is to allow for change in circumstances of employees that might have made them to change their mind and join the scheme. Within the three years window, employees who have changed their mind can approach their employers to join.

Although the amount of contributions into the schemes were phased out, as at 6th April 2019, total contributions into Auto-Enrolment scheme is 8% of member's income. The employee contribution is 4%, employer's contribution is 3% and government tax relief of 1% making a total of 8%.

Pension Freedoms

In 2015, the government introduced a new law that gave people greater access and flexibilities on how they access their Defined Contributions pension pots. Prior to this time, pensioners have limited options of how to draw down from their pensions which was mainly through annuity. However, with effect from 2015, the new rules have made provisions for flexibilities. The major aspect of this is that you no longer have to purchase annuity with your Defined Contributions pension pot. Options available to individuals apart from purchasing annuity are - leave the pension untouched, Flexible Access Drawdown (FAD), Uncrystallised Funds Pension Lump Sum, Cash in the whole pot, or mixtures of all of the options. With all of the options the 25% tax free lump sum is still available and the rest of the funds will be taxed at individual's marginal rate of tax, not 55% as in previous regime.

The major aspect of this is that you no longer have to purchase annuity with your Defined Contributions pension pot. Options available to individuals apart from purchasing annuity are - leave the pension untouched, Flexible Access Drawdown (FAD), Uncrystallised Funds Pension Lump Sum, Cash in the whole pot, or mixtures of all of the options.

Pension Transfers.

Pension Transfer simply provides an opportunity for individuals to transfer their pension from one scheme to the other or from one provider to the other. There are many reasons why people effect pension transfers. The most common transfers within the industry are transfers from Defined Benefit schemes to Defined Contributions schemes because of the newly introduced flexibility rules by the government. Individuals with Defined Benefits schemes who would like to access their pension funds with flexibilities will have to transfer such funds from the Defined Benefits scheme to Define Contribution scheme. However, most DB schemes have some statutory benefits, the pension transfer requires independent advice from qualified advisers within the industry. Transfer may not be suitable for some. The adviser would have to consider many factors including the individual's other assets available to fund income at retirement, need for guaranteed income, statutory increase of the DB scheme, need for flexibilities, personal circumstances including state of health etc. All these and many other soft facts are essential when considering Pension transfer. The adviser must be able to demonstrate that transfer is not disadvantageous to the individual in other to make transfer recommendation.

It must be noted that the value of the benefit is also important to determine whether independent advice is required. The triviality rules allow members to take their benefits as a lump sum if the total benefits in a defined benefit scheme is not more than £30,000. Under this rule, individual with small pots of £10,000 or less can combine three pots and commute as one lump sum.

For Trivial commutation therefore, an individual must be aged 55, or retiring early due to health reason and the total benefit from pension is not more than £30,000. For Small Pots, an individual must also be aged 55, or retiring early due to health reasons and pension benefits is not more than £10,000 in one pot.

Individuals with Defined Benefits schemes who would like to access their pension funds with flexibilities will have to transfer such funds from the Defined Benefits scheme to Define Contribution scheme.

Pension Options at Retirement.

At retirement, income from pension contributions depends on the type of scheme. Defined Benefits final salary scheme income and benefits are in line with the scheme rules and regulation. The scheme rules include retirement age, amount of lump sum and income based on number of years in employment, final salary at retirement. Also included in the scheme are statutory increase taking into consideration inflation. Members desiring flexibilities and control may consider transferring their benefits to defined contributions scheme as explained above.

Defined Contributions occupational pension and personal pension schemes income are based on the amount of funds available at retirement. During individual employee working years, their contributions and that of employers are invested by the pension provider to grow their funds to fund income at retirement. At retirement under the new rules, members are entitled to 25% of the pot as tax free lump sum while the remaining 75% is taxable at member's marginal rate of tax. Prior to the pension freedom regime, the only option available to individuals was to purchase annuity with the 75%. However, since the introduction of pension freedom, it's no longer compulsory to purchase annuities. Individuals now have flexibilities and options of how they draw down their pensions as mentioned above. The most suitable options would be based on member's situations and circumstances in addition to their financial objectives.

Chapter Action Points

***Join your workplace pension today if you haven't join yet and start making contributions.**

***Start a personal pension today if you're self-employed and not making any pension contributions now.**

***Seek professional advice to review any previous pension contributions in previous employment.**

SECTION THREE

CYCLE OF WEALTH VS CYCLE OF POVERTY

"THE RICH GETTING RICHER, THE POOR GETTING POORER"

CYCLE OF WEALTH VS CYCLE OF POVERTY

"THE RICH GETTING RICHER, THE POOR GETTING POORER"

I am sure you are familiar with the saying, *"the rich getting richer and the poor getting poorer"*. The secret behind this saying really lies in what the rich and the poor do with their resources. To strengthen the need for having solid financial plans and objectives and the benefits of seeking financial advice, I will illustrate with what I call The Cycle of Wealth and Cycle of Poverty shown below.

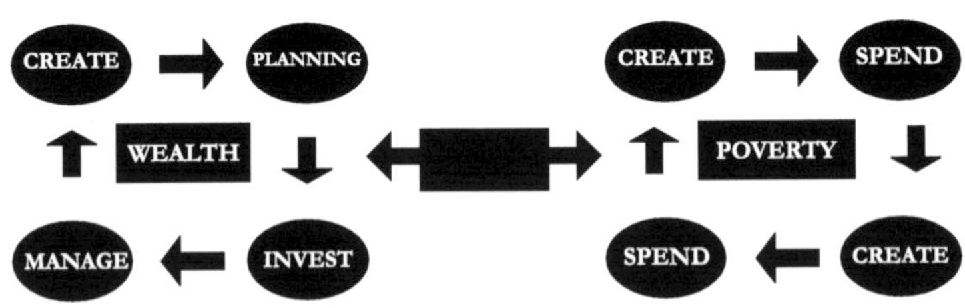

Fig 1 – *Wealth & Poverty Cycle*

Figure 5 above illustrates the gap between the rich and the poor. The difference lies in what they do with their resources.

Wealth vs Poverty Cycle

Stage 1 – Creating Wealth

Both the rich and the poor can create wealth. Having a means of income is the beginning of the journey for both of them. However, it is what people do with what they earn that determines where they end up-in wealth or poverty.

Generally, people make money or earn an income either through regular employment or business. It can also be through a combination of both. The poor focuses on working harder while the rich works smarter. I have met people doing two jobs and still not making much progress financially, while there are others with one job excelling with their financial plans. Again, the differentiator is what people do with what they earn. After creating financial resources through work or business, what next?

> *It is what people do with what they earn that determines where they end up- in wealth or poverty*

Stage 2 – Wealth Planning

While the rich are creating wealth, they also have some plans in place for what to do with their resources. The plan is a picture of their future financial desires which they have in mind and are working towards. Part of their earnings is allocated to this future. It doesn't matter how much, but the plan dictates and directs how they deploy their investable resources.

On the other side of the poverty cycle, after creating wealth, the poor moves to the 'spending' stage, without any plan. Apart from normal essential expenses, their disposable income is diverted towards unplanned spending on things that add no value to their financial future. Sadly, they keep up the cycle of creating and spending without anything substantial to show for their 'hard work'. When people are operating within the poverty cycle, you hear them say that their income is not enough to create wealth, or that they have so many financial commitments. They continue in what is described as the 'rat race', which gets them nowhere. If they however turn the table around, they will be able to move from operating in the poverty cycle to wealth cycle which requires sacrificing certain things today for a better tomorrow. Note, when there is no plan in place today for tomorrow, the future will be blank.

Financial planning will help you to be conscious of how your resources are deployed. It makes people to be intentional about creating wealth. The bitter truth is that, it is difficult to create wealth without being intentional about it. Even if you win the lottery and there is no plan, in a matter of time the wealth will fizzle away. There are many people who have come into sudden wealth and later returned to poverty because they failed to plan. Planning helps to eliminate wastage by focusing on priority. Some have miscellaneous spending that could be converted into investments with proper planning in place.

Planning helps you to see the future you want so you can work towards it. You know what your pension income will be when you retire. You know when and how your mortgage will be paid off. You know your family is financially secured if anything happens to you because you have put some family protection policies in place. You know your quality of life will not be affected if for any reason you are unable to carry out your own occupation due to prolonged ill-health, because you have put an income replacement policy in place. It is not enough to create wealth through employment or business income, there is need to properly plan how the resources will be utilised.

Your income is like a seed in your hand, you can either plant or eat it. A seed has the potential to become a forest if properly cultivated. When you eat your seed, you terminate the potential, but when you sow it, you activate that potential to bring forth more seed which eventually could become a forest. I love the story in the Holy Bible where Jesus told the parable of talents. A man gave his three servants some investable talents while he travelled, expecting that by the time of his return, there will be added profit. The Bible account said the master gave to each servant according to their ability. He gave five talents to one, two to another and one talent to the last one. This indicates that access to financial resources may not be the same, but we can start from where we are. The man who got five talents probably had ability for one but over the years he developed his capability to handle more. The same with the man with two talents. Sadly, the man with one talent did nothing to multiply his while the other two had made hundred percent returns. What is the difference between him and the others – **"planning"**. The other two servants went away and through planning invested the talents and made more talents while the servant with one talent just kept it safe and did not invest it.

Upon his return, the master commended the two servants who had multiplied their talents, but he condemned the unprofitable servant for not investing the money. Painfully, he gave instruction that what he had should be taken away from him and given to the servant who multiplied his five talents and now had ten. The servant ended up with nothing. When we fail to plan towards effective usage of our resources, what we have can be diminished in value or taken away from us somehow.

Looking deeper into the parable, when Jesus said *"For to everyone who has will more be given, and he will have an abundance. But from the one who has not, even what he has will be taken away" (Matt 25:29),* definitely He wasn't talking about talents because the master gave talents to every servant according to their abilities. What was lacking was the ability to think and plan how to multiply the resources in his hand. Instead, the servant concentrated on what his master would do if his investment failed and fear crept into his heart. I have met people who the fear of losing their money kept back from taking advantage of investment opportunities. The master said to the unprofitable servant, *"you could have sought professional advice to help you out. Yes, you may not know what to do, but you could have employed the services of someone who knows what to do."*

> *Note, when there is no plan in place today for tomorrow, the future will be blank.*

Stage 3 – Investment

Having put a plan in place for available resources, creating a better future requires that you make investment part of your plan. Certain percentage of any available resources must be targeted towards a better future. If nothing is allocated to this important aspect, then the future will be blank when you get there. The rich operating the wealth cycle always include investment in their planning. Investment gives you the opportunity to create the future of your dream. With investments, you are no longer just working for money but making money work for you. You are exploring avenues to add value to what you have. Your income from your employment may be limited but with strategic planning, potential income from your investment can be limitless. Part of proper planning is employing suitable investment for your identified objective.

Investment gives you the opportunity to create the future of your dream.

Going back to the parable of the talents, the master of the servant who did nothing to multiply his talent said to him, *'You wicked and slothful servant! You knew that I reap where I have not sown and gather where I scattered no seed?* [27] *Then you ought to have* invested *my money with the bankers, and at my coming I should have received what was my own with interest" (Matt 25:27).*

I want you to note that the master was not impressed with the servant keeping the money safe but preferred it was invested. Also, note that the master went away for a long time, which tells me that the ideal thing to do with long term financial objective is to consider investment, not just savings.

Stage 4 - Management

Having invested the resources, proper management is required. This stage is extremely crucial for a successful outcome. Investment management involves continuous monitoring of investments to ensure performance is on track to achieve set objective. Management requires the combined efforts of an adviser, an investment manager and an administrative management team.

If you put a pension policy in place at the age of thirty with a selected retirement age of sixty-five, the pension pot requires management for a period of thirty-five years. The objective is to ensure you have enough resources to fund your income at retirement. During the term of investments, many things can happen and impact the investment performance such as new government policies, changes in taxation, interest rates, market and economic policies, non-systemic factors, new legislation etc. All these and other factors require that the investment portfolios are properly managed to achieve successful outcomes. Through effective management, more wealth is created as the portfolio makes gains which are re-invested to make even more gains. This process continues over the time of investment.

This explains why rich continues to get richer while the poor continues to get poorer because they follow the poverty cycle. Individuals can break the poverty cycle by abandoning the 'create and spend' cycle and move to the 'create and plan' cycle.

Through effective management, more wealth is created as the investment portfolio makes gains which are re-invested in the portfolio to make even more gains. This process continues over the time of investment.

Majority of people operating the wealth cycle employ the services of professional financial advisers to achieve their investment objectives. The truth is, except you are qualified and authorised to practice within the industry, there is not much you can do for yourself with your financial plans and objectives due to regulatory framework in the United Kingdom. As I conclude, let me shed light on the role of financial advice in building wealth portfolio and achieving your financial objectives.

ROLES AND BENEFITS OF FINANCIAL ADVICE

The financial advisory industry in the United Kingdom under the watchdog of Financial Conduct Authority is a professional industry with high level of ethics and compliant procedure in place to protect customers. Before an individual can practice within the industry, certain qualifications are required by the regulator. In addition, most financial institutions also ensure their advisers have knowledge and experience before allowing them to engage with clients. The dynamism of the industry puts continuous professional development on top of sustainability of knowledge, making the industry attractive all over the world to investors. Qualified advisers in the United Kingdom are globally recognised and highly sought after in other parts of the world. The combination of the regulatory framework and qualitative professional advice gives investors confidence. They enjoy protection and to a large extent, they have peace of mind.

The roles played by these advisers and the benefits derived by investors are numerous. Let us examine some of them.

Education

One of the primary roles of a financial adviser is to keep clients abreast of what he or she is doing to help them achieve their financial objectives. The adviser educates clients about plan, process, implementation and monitoring of their investment. This way, they are updated about their investment portfolios as the adviser periodically reviews the portfolio for them. Clients also have the opportunity to ask questions about their investments, increasing their knowledge. The more people are informed, the more committed they are to the process. When clients are not well informed, they become either demotivated or have wrong expectations. The demotivated ones give up, while the ones with wrong expectations end up being disappointed.

The adviser educates the client about plan, process, implementation and monitoring of their investment

Investment Risk Management

Building an investment portfolio involves risk. Since we cannot eliminate risk totally from investment, it is important that the level of risk involved in an investor's portfolio is in line with their risk profile, thus keeping them in a safe environment. It is also important to ascertain that the level of risk taken is commensurate with the returns of the investments. Monitoring and managing the risks associated with client's investment portfolio is a crucial duty of the financial adviser so as to ensure best outcome.

Determining the risk profile of an investor requires that the adviser takes the client through a fact-finding exercise to obtain comprehensive information about his or her investment objectives. This helps to assess client's risk profile, taking into consideration their attitude to risk and capacity for loss. The exercise helps in determining suitable investment vehicle and portfolio to achieve client's objectives.

When considering risk management in investment, in addition to the possibility that investment may fall in value, other risks to be considered is the likelihood that the value of investment may not rise with inflation, thereby eroding the value of capital over a period of time. It is important that funds are invested in such a way that the buying power doesn't depreciate over the investment period. Another risk to consider are access to funds when needed. The financial adviser must consider the ease of access to investment portfolio without penalties. This is because some investment vehicles attract withdrawal charges if the client has to make a withdrawal earlier than scheduled in the investment. Also, some investments may be difficult to sell without resulting in loss in value if the investor is desperate for money. The client's ability to withstand a fall in value of investment should also be considered by the adviser, especially for investors who depend on income from their investment portfolios. A fall in the value of investment will automatically results in fall in the level of income. These and other factors are what the adviser put into consideration and tries to manage in the best interest of the client. Without doubt, the role of an advisor in proper risk management cannot and should not be taken for granted.

Since we cannot eliminate risk totally from investment, it is important that the level of risk involved in an investor's portfolio is in line with their risk profile, thus keeping them in a safe environment.

Safety

Unfortunately, all industries have bad eggs and the financial services industry in the UK is not exempted. There are many 'cowboy' advisers in the industry who are mainly interested in the amount of money they can make from ignorant investors. Many of these folks operate outside of the regulatory frameworks and therefore offer all sorts of non-regulatory products with promises of attractive returns to investors. In these cases, investors are not protected, which means if anything goes wrong, they have no protection or compensation to fall back on. A regulated adviser operates within the regulatory framework with adequate complain and compensation procedure in place should anything go wrong. Each advisory firm is expected to incorporate complain and compensation procedure in their service disclosure document. Within the document, clients are advised about the complaint procedure, including details of the Financial Ombudsman Services (FOS) and Financial Compensation Schemes (FCS). In the event of a complaint being upheld by the FOS, client will receive compensation in line with the industry's compensation scheme. Such safety is what makes taking financial advice of great value.

Investment Research

Not many investors have the time to research the market for suitable products to achieve their objectives, and even if they did, the task of identifying the ideal investment out of thousands of products is herculean. Investment research in a complex industry like financial advisory services is a major task. Different providers have different products with different features and charges. The tools to bring thousands of products together for comparison is not always available to individuals. Also, past performance is not indicative of future returns, therefore investors cannot just rely on past performances to make decision. Other factors must also be taken into consideration during the research being carried out by the adviser, to justify their decision and selection of how they can add value to the investment portfolio. The financial adviser is not only qualified, he understands different investment options. He knows what to look for in each investment opportunity. He is able to carry out thorough research and advise clients adequately in line with their investment objectives.

Also, past performance is not indicative of future returns, therefore investors cannot just rely on past performances to make decision.

Value

Seeking financial advice in building your wealth portfolio and achieving set financial objectives is a value adding exercise. Research has revealed that individuals who employ the services of financial advisers have overall higher rate of returns in their portfolios compared to do-it-yourself individuals. However, it must be emphasised that adding value is not just about picking the best investments, but rather considering other factors that influence overall returns in a portfolio, which if ignored, can lead to a costly mistake. Examples of such factors are asset allocation, tax implications, investment costs, on-going review and rebalancing, income or capital needs, exit strategy, etc.

In investment, having the right asset allocation that represents client's risk profile is crucial. Assigning different percentages of client's funds to different asset classes– cash, bonds, properties, equities and alternative investments in such a way that they all add great value to the entire portfolio is the professional responsibility of the adviser. It requires skills and knowledge which must be demonstrated in establishing client's objectives and goals alongside risk profile.

Another crucial aspect to consider in putting an investment portfolio in place is tax planning. An individual's tax status has great impact on the entire investment portfolio; therefore, consideration must be given to tax implications on investments and policies to mitigate against liabilities. Different investmcnts and policies have different tax charges adduced to them, such as income tax, capital gain tax and inheritance tax liabilities. A lot of people have no clue what tax applies to which investments. There are tax-free and tax-efficient investment portfolios such as ISA's and Pensions, but not everyone is aware of this. Many clients don't know the difference and how it affects their financial plans. They fail to utilise these allowances and proceed to put money in other investment with tax liabilities. With proper advice, they would have been guided on how to maximise these opportunities which can add value to their wealth proposition.

Charges within investment portfolio have great impact on the overall returns of the portfolio. As can be expected, deducted charges reduce the value of returns of the portfolio. Although all possible charges are made known to investors at point of engagements, the overall impact on medium to long term is not known at the onset, therefore advisers constantly monitor the impact of costs on portfolio alongside on-going review with the intention of ensuring value for money.

Annually, advisers will have on-going review sessions with the clients as part of service proposition, except otherwise declined by the client. The essence of the review is to ensure the portfolio is on track to achieve client's objectives and goals. The review provides opportunity to make necessary adjustments by rebalancing the portfolio in line with client's risk profile.

There are instances where a client has need for income or capital at a particular point in time. How to plan ahead and meet such needs without disrupting the entire portfolio requires professional input. In constructing and managing the portfolio, advisers will ensure such income and capital can be drawn in such a way that it will not create additional tax liabilities or incur an exit penalty within the portfolio.

Considering all the reasons mentioned above and many more, it becomes obvious that engaging the services of professional advisers in building your wealth portfolio is a better concept to adopt for suitable and fulfilling outcome.

Seeking financial advice in building wealth portfolio and achieving financial objectives is a value adding exercise.

Chapter Action Points

*** Decide to start building your wealth portfolio today.**

*** Seek immediate financial advice to identify the most suitable place to commence based on available resources.**

*** Make up your mind to sacrifice some pleasures today for a better tomorrow.**

*** Be comfortable with plans, objectives and recommendations by your adviser.**

*** Be committed to the plans and objectives.**

*** Always keep your adviser informed of any changes in your plans and objectives before you take any action. He may have a better way of managing the changes.**

APPENDIX

Mortgage Illustration

This document was produced for Mr Niyi Murele on 13/04/2022.
This document was produced on the basis of the information that you have provided so far and on the current financial market conditions.
The information below remains valid until 13/04/2022. After that date, it may change in line with market conditions.
This document does not constitute an obligation for Danske Bank to grant you a loan.

1. Lender
Danske Bank Telephone Number: 0345 600 5775 PO Box 183 Donegall Square West Belfast BT1 6JS

2. Credit intermediary
Kingdom Wealth Management The Haven Carrs Drive HIGH WYCOMBE, Buckinghamshire UK HP12 4BT Contact: Niyi Murele Telephone Number: 07930 313159 Kingdom Wealth Management recommend, having assessed your needs and circumstances, that you take out this mortgage. Kingdom Wealth Management's fees are described in section 4. Danske Bank will pay St James's Place Wealth Management, L & G Mortgage Club and Kingdom Wealth Management an amount of £900.00 in cash and benefits if you take out this mortgage.

3. Main features of the loan

Product: Intermediary 2 Year Fixed Fee Paying Carbon Neutral (Purchase) £150k+

Amount and currency of the loan to be granted: £225,000.00 plus £999.00 for fees that will be added to the loan.
Duration of the loan: 25 years

This is a capital repayment mortgage subject to a variable interest rate. This mortgage initially has a fixed rate until 01/07/2024.

Total amount to be repaid: £346,767.00

This amount is illustrative and may vary, in particular in relation with the variation of the interest rate.

Please refer to the lender for further details.

This means you will pay back £1.53 for every £1 borrowed.

Value of the property assumed to prepare this information sheet: £250,000.00.
Maximum available loan amount relative to the value of the property: 90.00%.
The maximum theoretically possible to borrow would be £225,000.00

This loan will be secured against the property.

4. Interest rate and other costs

The annual percentage rate of charge (APRC) is the total cost of the loan expressed as an annual percentage. The APRC is provided to help you compare different offers. The APRC applicable to your loan is 3.7%

It comprises:

Interest rate

- A fixed rate of 2.21% until 01/07/2024
- Followed by Danske Bank Reference Rate (UK) plus a margin of 3.20%. Danske Bank Reference Rate (UK) is a variable rate which is currently 0.75%, giving a current rate payable of 3.95% for the remaining term of the mortgage

Costs to be paid on a one-off basis

Product Fee which is payable to Danske Bank when your mortgage completes. This fee is not refundable. This fee will be added to your mortgage.	£999.00
Valuation Fee which is payable to your valuer on application. This fee is payable by you to the professional valuer when we instruct him. This is the cost of obtaining a mortgage valuation over the property that is being offered as Security to the Bank. The valuation fee is non refundable. This fee only covers the cost of a mortgage valuation report. It is not a survey report and is prepared solely for the benefit of the Bank. If you require a full survey report then you will have to request that yourself and the valuer will provide you with an estimate of the likely fee. This fee is not refundable.	£225.00
Vacate Mortgage Fee which is payable to Danske Bank when the loan is repaid in full. This fee is not refundable. The figure quoted here is the current fee amount which may change.	£50.00
Deeds Release Fee which is payable to Danske Bank when the loan is repaid in full. This fee is not refundable. The figure quoted here is the current fee amount which may change.	£75.00

Costs to be paid regularly

None

This APRC is calculated using assumptions regarding the interest rate. We assume any variable interest rate remains at the interest rate shown above and that any estimated fees remain unchanged. Because your loan is a variable interest rate loan, the actual APRC could be different from this APRC if the interest rate for your loan changes. For example, if the interest rate rose to 8.45%, the APRC could increase to 8.9%.

Please make sure you are aware of all other taxes and costs associated with your loan.

5. Frequency and number of payments

Repayment frequency: Monthly

Number of payments: 300

6. Amount of each instalment

25 monthly payments at a fixed rate of 2.21%	£981.18
Followed by:	
275 monthly payments at a variable rate, currently 3.95%	£1,170.50

All payments must be made in pound sterling.

Your income may change. Please consider whether you will still be able to afford your monthly repayment instalments if your income falls.

The interest rate on this loan can change. This means the amount of your monthly instalments could increase or decrease. For example, if the interest rate rose to 8.45%, your payments could increase to £1,812.20.

7. Additional obligations

The borrower must comply with the following obligations in order to benefit from the lending conditions described in this document.

The property must be insured against all normal risks for its full reinstatement value for the duration of the loan. You are not obliged to buy this insurance from us.

You must not lease or otherwise dispose of any part of the Security during the loan without our written consent.

You must comply with any additional obligations we may seek to impose following credit assessment. Some of these obligations may be required to be fulfilled before the loan is drawn down and other obligations may apply for the duration of the loan.

Please note that the lending conditions described in this document (including the interest rate) may change if these obligations are not complied with.

8. Early repayment

You have the possibility to repay this loan early, either fully or partially.

Early repayment charge

Loan amount	Basis of the charge	Date of repayment	Maximum amount of charge
£225,999.00	4.00% of the amount repaid	until 01/07/2022	£9,039.96
£225,434.03	3.00% of the amount repaid	until 03/07/2023	£6,763.02
£217,994.10	2.00% of the amount repaid	until 01/07/2024	£4,359.88

You will have to pay the following fees on early repayment:
Vacate Mortgage Fee: (currently) £50.00
Deeds Release Fee: (currently) £75.00
The maximum charge you could pay to repay your mortgage is £9,039.96 plus fees, which are currently £125.00.

Should you decide to repay this loan early, please contact us to ascertain the exact level of the early repayment charge at that moment.

9. Flexible features

PORTABILITY

This mortgage contract is portable if you choose to move house. You are allowed to retain your product, if Danske Bank agree to a new home loan, for the outstanding balance at that point in time. The Terms and Conditions for your product will continue to apply until the end of any Special or Concessionary Rate Period. See "Home Loans General Offer Conditions" documentation where appropriate for further details regarding conditions and restrictions.

ADDITIONAL FEATURES

Overpayments

Overpay (Making a lump sum repayment during the Fixed Rate Period) You can make a lump sum overpayment during the Fixed Rate Period without incurring an Early Repayment Charge provided the overpayment:
• Is a maximum of 10.00% of the outstanding balance of your loan;
•Is made by way of a one off lump sum overpayment; and
•Is made once during any calendar year being the period from 1 January to 31 December In all other cases.
The Early Repayment Charge referred to in the "Early Repayment" section will apply to any additional lump sum overpayment. Once we receive the lump sum overpayment, the outstanding loan balance and the amount of interest payable, will be reduced immediately. This ensures that you benefit straight away. There will be no changes made to the expiry date of your loan, the Fixed Interest Rate or the amount of the Instalment Payment during the Fixed Rate Period. This means that your monthly repayments will continue to be based off your original loan amount for the Fixed Rate Period. At the end of the Fixed Rate Period, we will recalculate the new Instalment Payment amount based on the outstanding loan balance and remaining term of your loan at that time. The remaining term of the loan will not be reduced automatically. If you want to reduce the remaining term of your loan then you should contact us. At the end of the Fixed Rate Period, you can make regular overpayments or lump sum overpayments and the section titled 'Payments' of the 'Home Loan General Offer Conditions' will apply. If you want to make a lump sum overpayment during the Fixed Rate Period, you should contact us via secure mail or telephone. The funds being used to make any lump sum overpayment must be available in the Danske Bank account used to service your loan.

10. Other rights of the borrower

You have 7 days after you have been given a binding mortgage offer to reflect before committing yourself to taking out this loan.

Once the mortgage contract is concluded you cannot withdraw from the contract but you can repay it at any time in accordance with the terms of the mortgage contract.

11. Complaints

If you wish to register a complaint, please.

Call us on 01285 878 201 between 0800 and 1700 Monday to Friday

Send an email to client.liaison@sjp.co.uk

You will receive an immediate return email acknowledgement confirming we have received your email.
We will also send you a formal written acknowledgement with a personal contact name for future communications.

Write to us at:
Client Liaison
St. James's Place Wealth Management
1 Tetbury Rd
Cirencester
Gloucestershire
GL7 1FP

If we do not resolve the complaint to your satisfaction internally, you can also contact:
The Financial Ombudsman Service
Telephone Number: 0800 023 4567
Website: http://www.financial-ombudsman.org.uk/

12. Non-compliance with the commitments linked to the loan: consequences for the borrower
Danske Bank will provide you with a copy of our document entitled 'Home Loan General Offer Conditions' which will apply to this mortgage. This document will provide you with full details of your obligations under the contract. Danske Bank set out below the different main cases where a failure to comply with your obligations under the contract may have financial or legal consequences for you: • If you do not make the required repayments when they fall due - Danske Bank may demand repayment of the full amount outstanding. This may mean that you will incur further interest and costs. Danske Bank may also pass information to credit reference agencies which may impact on your ability to take out further loans. Continuing to miss payments under the contract may ultimately lead to Danske Bank taking action to repossess your home. • If you do not keep the property described as Security in a good state of repair - Danske Bank may require you to take action to remedy any damage which has been caused to the property. If the value of the property has been reduced as a result of your failure to keep the property in a good state of repair Danske Bank may decide to take action to carry out repairs to the property and to debit our costs to your loan account. • If you do not keep the property described as Security insured to its full reinstatement value during the term of the loan - Danske Bank may decide to insure the property and debit our costs to your loan account. For further information on the consequences of non-compliance please see Danske Bank's lending conditions by referring to the Terms and Conditions document provided with your mortgage offer. Should you encounter difficulties in making your monthly payments, please contact Danske Bank straight away to explore possible solutions. **As a last resort, your home may be repossessed if you do not keep up with payments.**

13. Additional information
Danske Bank will give you a draft credit agreement when they give you a binding mortgage offer.

14. Supervisor
This lender is supervised by the Financial Conduct Authority - www.fca.org.uk This credit intermediary is supervised by the Financial Conduct Authority - www.fca.org.uk

Payment Schedule

The monthly payments could be considerably different to those shown, due to variable interest rates

#	Date	Rate	Rate type	Payment	Paid to date	Interest charged to date	Principal repaid	Remaining principal
1	Jun - 2022	2.21%	FIXED	£981.18	£981.18	£416.21	£564.97	£225,434.03
2	Jul - 2022	2.21%	FIXED	£981.18	£1,962.36	£831.39	£1,130.97	£224,868.03
3	Aug - 2022	2.21%	FIXED	£981.18	£2,943.54	£1,245.52	£1,698.02	£224,300.98
4	Sep - 2022	2.21%	FIXED	£981.18	£3,924.72	£1,658.61	£2,266.11	£223,732.89
5	Oct - 2022	2.21%	FIXED	£981.18	£4,905.90	£2,070.65	£2,835.25	£223,163.75
6	Nov - 2022	2.21%	FIXED	£981.18	£5,887.08	£2,481.64	£3,405.44	£222,593.56
7	Dec - 2022	2.21%	FIXED	£981.18	£6,868.26	£2,891.59	£3,976.67	£222,022.33
8	Jan - 2023	2.21%	FIXED	£981.18	£7,849.44	£3,300.46	£4,548.98	£221,450.04
9	Feb - 2023	2.21%	FIXED	£981.18	£8,830.62	£3,708.31	£5,122.30	£220,876.70
10	Mar - 2023	2.21%	FIXED	£981.18	£9,811.80	£4,115.10	£5,696.70	£220,302.30
11	Apr - 2023	2.21%	FIXED	£981.18	£10,792.98	£4,520.82	£6,272.16	£219,726.84
12	May - 2023	2.21%	FIXED	£981.18	£11,774.16	£4,925.48	£6,848.68	£219,150.32
13	Jun - 2023	2.21%	FIXED	£981.18	£12,755.34	£5,329.08	£7,426.25	£218,572.75
14	Jul - 2023	2.21%	FIXED	£981.18	£13,736.52	£5,731.62	£8,004.90	£217,994.10
15	Aug - 2023	2.21%	FIXED	£981.18	£14,717.70	£6,133.10	£8,584.60	£217,414.40
16	Sep - 2023	2.21%	FIXED	£981.18	£15,698.88	£6,533.50	£9,165.38	£216,833.62
17	Oct - 2023	2.21%	FIXED	£981.18	£16,680.06	£6,932.84	£9,747.22	£216,251.78
18	Nov - 2023	2.21%	FIXED	£981.18	£17,661.24	£7,331.10	£10,330.14	£215,668.86
19	Dec - 2023	2.21%	FIXED	£981.18	£18,642.42	£7,728.29	£10,914.13	£215,084.87
20	Jan - 2024	2.21%	FIXED	£981.18	£19,623.60	£8,124.40	£11,499.20	£214,499.80
21	Feb - 2024	2.21%	FIXED	£981.18	£20,604.78	£8,519.44	£12,085.34	£213,913.66
22	Mar - 2024	2.21%	FIXED	£981.18	£21,585.96	£8,913.40	£12,672.56	£213,326.44
23	Apr - 2024	2.21%	FIXED	£981.18	£22,567.14	£9,306.28	£13,260.86	£212,738.14
24	May - 2024	2.21%	FIXED	£981.18	£23,548.32	£9,698.07	£13,850.25	£212,148.75
25	Jun - 2024	2.21%	FIXED	£981.18	£24,529.50	£10,088.78	£14,440.72	£211,558.28
26	Jul - 2024	3.95%	VARIABLE	£1,170.50	£25,700.00	£10,785.15	£14,914.85	£211,084.15
27	Aug - 2024	3.95%	VARIABLE	£1,170.50	£26,870.50	£11,479.97	£15,390.53	£210,608.47
28	Sep - 2024	3.95%	VARIABLE	£1,170.50	£28,041.00	£12,173.23	£15,867.78	£210,131.22
29	Oct - 2024	3.95%	VARIABLE	£1,170.50	£29,211.50	£12,864.91	£16,346.60	£209,652.40
30	Nov - 2024	3.95%	VARIABLE	£1,170.50	£30,382.00	£13,555.01	£16,827.00	£209,172.00
31	Dec - 2024	3.95%	VARIABLE	£1,170.50	£31,552.50	£14,243.54	£17,308.97	£208,690.03
32	Jan - 2025	3.95%	VARIABLE	£1,170.50	£32,723.00	£14,930.48	£17,792.54	£208,206.46
33	Feb - 2025	3.95%	VARIABLE	£1,170.50	£33,893.50	£15,615.82	£18,277.69	£207,721.31
34	Mar - 2025	3.95%	VARIABLE	£1,170.50	£35,064.00	£16,299.57	£18,764.45	£207,234.55
35	Apr - 2025	3.95%	VARIABLE	£1,170.50	£36,234.50	£16,981.72	£19,252.80	£206,746.20
36	May - 2025	3.95%	VARIABLE	£1,170.50	£37,405.00	£17,662.28	£19,742.76	£206,256.24
37	Jun - 2025	3.95%	VARIABLE	£1,170.50	£38,575.50	£18,341.19	£20,234.34	£205,764.66
38	Jul - 2025	3.95%	VARIABLE	£1,170.50	£39,746.00	£19,018.49	£20,727.53	£205,271.47
39	Aug - 2025	3.95%	VARIABLE	£1,170.50	£40,916.50	£19,694.18	£21,222.35	£204,776.65
40	Sep - 2025	3.95%	VARIABLE	£1,170.50	£42,087.00	£20,368.24	£21,718.79	£204,280.21
41	Oct - 2025	3.95%	VARIABLE	£1,170.50	£43,257.50	£21,040.66	£22,216.67	£203,782.13
42	Nov - 2025	3.95%	VARIABLE	£1,170.50	£44,428.00	£21,711.44	£22,716.59	£203,282.41
43	Dec - 2025	3.95%	VARIABLE	£1,170.50	£45,598.50	£22,380.58	£23,217.96	£202,781.04
44	Jan - 2026	3.95%	VARIABLE	£1,170.50	£46,769.00	£23,048.07	£23,720.97	£202,278.03
45	Feb - 2026	3.95%	VARIABLE	£1,170.50	£47,939.50	£23,713.90	£24,225.64	£201,773.36
46	Mar - 2026	3.95%	VARIABLE	£1,170.50	£49,110.00	£24,378.07	£24,731.97	£201,267.03
47	Apr - 2026	3.95%	VARIABLE	£1,170.50	£50,280.50	£25,040.57	£25,239.97	£200,759.03
48	May - 2026	3.95%	VARIABLE	£1,170.50	£51,451.00	£25,701.40	£25,749.64	£200,249.36
49	Jun - 2026	3.95%	VARIABLE	£1,170.50	£52,621.50	£26,360.56	£26,260.99	£199,738.01
50	Jul - 2026	3.95%	VARIABLE	£1,170.50	£53,792.00	£27,018.03	£26,774.02	£199,224.98
51	Aug - 2026	3.95%	VARIABLE	£1,170.50	£54,962.50	£27,673.81	£27,288.74	£198,710.26
52	Sep - 2026	3.95%	VARIABLE	£1,170.50	£56,133.00	£28,327.90	£27,805.16	£198,193.84
53	Oct - 2026	3.95%	VARIABLE	£1,170.50	£57,303.50	£28,980.29	£28,323.27	£197,675.73
54	Nov - 2026	3.95%	VARIABLE	£1,170.50	£58,474.00	£29,630.97	£28,843.09	£197,155.91
55	Dec - 2026	3.95%	VARIABLE	£1,170.50	£59,644.50	£30,279.94	£29,364.62	£196,634.38
56	Jan - 2027	3.95%	VARIABLE	£1,170.50	£60,815.00	£30,927.20	£29,887.87	£196,111.13
57	Feb - 2027	3.95%	VARIABLE	£1,170.50	£61,985.50	£31,572.73	£30,412.84	£195,586.16
58	Mar - 2027	3.95%	VARIABLE	£1,170.50	£63,156.00	£32,216.53	£30,939.53	£195,059.47
59	Apr - 2027	3.95%	VARIABLE	£1,170.50	£64,326.50	£32,858.60	£31,467.97	£194,531.03
60	May - 2027	3.95%	VARIABLE	£1,170.50	£65,497.00	£33,498.94	£31,998.14	£194,000.86
61	Jun - 2027	3.95%	VARIABLE	£1,170.50	£66,667.50	£34,137.52	£32,530.05	£193,466.95

62	Jul - 2027	3.95%	VARIABLE	£1,170.50	£67,838.00	£34,774.36	£33,063.72	£192,935.28
63	Aug - 2027	3.95%	VARIABLE	£1,170.50	£69,008.50	£35,409.44	£33,599.14	£192,399.86
64	Sep - 2027	3.95%	VARIABLE	£1,170.50	£70,179.00	£36,042.75	£34,136.33	£191,862.67
65	Oct - 2027	3.95%	VARIABLE	£1,170.50	£71,349.50	£36,674.30	£34,675.28	£191,323.72
66	Nov - 2027	3.95%	VARIABLE	£1,170.50	£72,520.00	£37,304.07	£35,216.01	£190,782.99
67	Dec - 2027	3.95%	VARIABLE	£1,170.50	£73,690.50	£37,932.07	£35,758.52	£190,240.48
68	Jan - 2028	3.95%	VARIABLE	£1,170.50	£74,861.00	£38,558.28	£36,302.81	£189,696.19
69	Feb - 2028	3.95%	VARIABLE	£1,170.50	£76,031.50	£39,182.69	£36,848.90	£189,150.10
70	Mar - 2028	3.95%	VARIABLE	£1,170.50	£77,202.00	£39,805.31	£37,396.78	£188,602.22
71	Apr - 2028	3.95%	VARIABLE	£1,170.50	£78,372.50	£40,426.13	£37,946.47	£188,052.53
72	May - 2028	3.95%	VARIABLE	£1,170.50	£79,543.00	£41,045.13	£38,497.96	£187,501.04
73	Jun - 2028	3.95%	VARIABLE	£1,170.50	£80,713.50	£41,662.32	£39,051.28	£186,947.72
74	Jul - 2028	3.95%	VARIABLE	£1,170.50	£81,884.00	£42,277.89	£39,606.41	£186,392.59
75	Aug - 2028	3.95%	VARIABLE	£1,170.50	£83,054.50	£42,891.24	£40,163.37	£185,835.63
76	Sep - 2028	3.95%	VARIABLE	£1,170.50	£84,225.00	£43,502.85	£40,722.16	£185,276.84
77	Oct - 2028	3.95%	VARIABLE	£1,170.50	£85,395.50	£44,112.82	£41,282.79	£184,716.21
78	Nov - 2028	3.95%	VARIABLE	£1,170.50	£86,566.00	£44,720.84	£41,845.27	£184,153.73
79	Dec - 2028	3.95%	VARIABLE	£1,170.50	£87,736.50	£45,327.01	£42,409.60	£183,589.40
80	Jan - 2029	3.95%	VARIABLE	£1,170.50	£88,907.00	£45,931.33	£42,975.79	£183,023.21
81	Feb - 2029	3.95%	VARIABLE	£1,170.50	£90,077.50	£46,533.76	£43,543.84	£182,455.16
82	Mar - 2029	3.95%	VARIABLE	£1,170.50	£91,248.00	£47,134.36	£44,113.76	£181,885.24
83	Apr - 2029	3.95%	VARIABLE	£1,170.50	£92,418.50	£47,733.07	£44,685.56	£181,313.44
84	May - 2029	3.95%	VARIABLE	£1,170.50	£93,589.00	£48,329.89	£45,259.23	£180,739.77
85	Jun - 2029	3.95%	VARIABLE	£1,170.50	£94,759.50	£48,924.82	£45,834.80	£180,164.20
86	Jul - 2029	3.95%	VARIABLE	£1,170.50	£95,930.00	£49,517.86	£46,412.26	£179,586.74
87	Aug - 2029	3.95%	VARIABLE	£1,170.50	£97,100.50	£50,109.00	£46,991.63	£179,007.37
88	Sep - 2029	3.95%	VARIABLE	£1,170.50	£98,271.00	£50,698.24	£47,572.89	£178,426.11
89	Oct - 2029	3.95%	VARIABLE	£1,170.50	£99,441.50	£51,285.56	£48,156.08	£177,842.92
90	Nov - 2029	3.95%	VARIABLE	£1,170.50	£100,612.00	£51,870.96	£48,741.18	£177,257.82
91	Dec - 2029	3.95%	VARIABLE	£1,170.50	£101,782.50	£52,454.43	£49,328.21	£176,670.79
92	Jan - 2030	3.95%	VARIABLE	£1,170.50	£102,953.00	£53,035.97	£49,917.17	£176,081.83
93	Feb - 2030	3.95%	VARIABLE	£1,170.50	£104,123.50	£53,615.57	£50,508.07	£175,490.93
94	Mar - 2030	3.95%	VARIABLE	£1,170.50	£105,294.00	£54,193.23	£51,100.91	£174,898.09
95	Apr - 2030	3.95%	VARIABLE	£1,170.50	£106,464.50	£54,768.94	£51,695.71	£174,303.29
96	May - 2030	3.95%	VARIABLE	£1,170.50	£107,635.00	£55,342.69	£52,292.46	£173,706.54
97	Jun - 2030	3.95%	VARIABLE	£1,170.50	£108,805.50	£55,914.47	£52,891.18	£173,107.82
98	Jul - 2030	3.95%	VARIABLE	£1,170.50	£109,976.00	£56,484.28	£53,491.87	£172,507.13
99	Aug - 2030	3.95%	VARIABLE	£1,170.50	£111,146.50	£57,052.12	£54,094.54	£171,904.46
100	Sep - 2030	3.95%	VARIABLE	£1,170.50	£112,317.00	£57,617.97	£54,699.19	£171,299.81
101	Oct - 2030	3.95%	VARIABLE	£1,170.50	£113,487.50	£58,181.83	£55,305.83	£170,693.17
102	Nov - 2030	3.95%	VARIABLE	£1,170.50	£114,658.00	£58,743.70	£55,914.46	£170,084.54
103	Dec - 2030	3.95%	VARIABLE	£1,170.50	£115,828.50	£59,303.56	£56,525.10	£169,473.90
104	Jan - 2031	3.95%	VARIABLE	£1,170.50	£116,999.00	£59,861.41	£57,137.75	£168,861.25
105	Feb - 2031	3.95%	VARIABLE	£1,170.50	£118,169.50	£60,417.25	£57,752.42	£168,246.58
106	Mar - 2031	3.95%	VARIABLE	£1,170.50	£119,340.00	£60,971.06	£58,369.11	£167,629.89
107	Apr - 2031	3.95%	VARIABLE	£1,170.50	£120,510.50	£61,522.84	£58,987.83	£167,011.17
108	May - 2031	3.95%	VARIABLE	£1,170.50	£121,681.00	£62,072.58	£59,608.59	£166,390.41
109	Jun - 2031	3.95%	VARIABLE	£1,170.50	£122,851.50	£62,620.29	£60,231.39	£165,767.61
110	Jul - 2031	3.95%	VARIABLE	£1,170.50	£124,022.00	£63,165.94	£60,856.24	£165,142.76
111	Aug - 2031	3.95%	VARIABLE	£1,170.50	£125,192.50	£63,709.53	£61,483.15	£164,515.85
112	Sep - 2031	3.95%	VARIABLE	£1,170.50	£126,363.00	£64,251.06	£62,112.12	£163,886.88
113	Oct - 2031	3.95%	VARIABLE	£1,170.50	£127,533.50	£64,790.53	£62,743.16	£163,255.84
114	Nov - 2031	3.95%	VARIABLE	£1,170.50	£128,704.00	£65,327.91	£63,376.28	£162,622.72
115	Dec - 2031	3.95%	VARIABLE	£1,170.50	£129,874.50	£65,863.21	£64,011.48	£161,987.52
116	Jan - 2032	3.95%	VARIABLE	£1,170.50	£131,045.00	£66,396.42	£64,648.77	£161,350.23
117	Feb - 2032	3.95%	VARIABLE	£1,170.50	£132,215.50	£66,927.53	£65,288.16	£160,710.84
118	Mar - 2032	3.95%	VARIABLE	£1,170.50	£133,386.00	£67,456.54	£65,929.66	£160,069.34
119	Apr - 2032	3.95%	VARIABLE	£1,170.50	£134,556.50	£67,983.43	£66,573.27	£159,425.73
120	May - 2032	3.95%	VARIABLE	£1,170.50	£135,727.00	£68,508.21	£67,218.99	£158,780.01
121	Jun - 2032	3.95%	VARIABLE	£1,170.50	£136,897.50	£69,030.86	£67,866.84	£158,132.16
122	Jul - 2032	3.95%	VARIABLE	£1,170.50	£138,068.00	£69,551.38	£68,516.83	£157,482.17
123	Aug - 2032	3.95%	VARIABLE	£1,170.50	£139,238.50	£70,069.75	£69,168.95	£156,830.05
124	Sep - 2032	3.95%	VARIABLE	£1,170.50	£140,409.00	£70,585.99	£69,823.22	£156,175.78
125	Oct - 2032	3.95%	VARIABLE	£1,170.50	£141,579.50	£71,100.07	£70,479.64	£155,519.36
126	Nov - 2032	3.95%	VARIABLE	£1,170.50	£142,750.00	£71,611.98	£71,138.23	£154,860.77
127	Dec - 2032	3.95%	VARIABLE	£1,170.50	£143,920.50	£72,121.73	£71,798.98	£154,200.02
128	Jan - 2033	3.95%	VARIABLE	£1,170.50	£145,091.00	£72,628.31	£72,461.91	£153,537.09

129	Feb - 2033	3.95%	VARIABLE	£1,170.50	£146,261.50	£73,134.70	£73,127.02	£152,871.98
130	Mar - 2033	3.95%	VARIABLE	£1,170.50	£147,432.00	£73,637.91	£73,794.31	£152,204.69
131	Apr - 2033	3.95%	VARIABLE	£1,170.50	£148,602.50	£74,138.91	£74,463.81	£151,535.19
132	May - 2033	3.95%	VARIABLE	£1,170.50	£149,773.00	£74,637.72	£75,135.51	£150,863.49
133	Jun - 2033	3.95%	VARIABLE	£1,170.50	£150,943.50	£75,134.31	£75,809.42	£150,189.58
134	Jul - 2033	3.95%	VARIABLE	£1,170.50	£152,114.00	£75,628.68	£76,485.55	£149,513.45
135	Aug - 2033	3.95%	VARIABLE	£1,170.50	£153,284.50	£76,120.83	£77,163.90	£148,835.10
136	Sep - 2033	3.95%	VARIABLE	£1,170.50	£154,455.00	£76,610.75	£77,844.49	£148,154.51
137	Oct - 2033	3.95%	VARIABLE	£1,170.50	£155,625.50	£77,098.42	£78,527.31	£147,471.69
138	Nov - 2033	3.95%	VARIABLE	£1,170.50	£156,796.00	£77,583.85	£79,212.39	£146,786.61
139	Dec - 2033	3.95%	VARIABLE	£1,170.50	£157,966.50	£78,067.02	£79,899.72	£146,099.28
140	Jan - 2034	3.95%	VARIABLE	£1,170.50	£159,137.00	£78,547.93	£80,589.31	£145,409.69
141	Feb - 2034	3.95%	VARIABLE	£1,170.50	£160,307.50	£79,026.57	£81,281.17	£144,717.83
142	Mar - 2034	3.95%	VARIABLE	£1,170.50	£161,478.00	£79,502.93	£81,975.31	£144,023.69
143	Apr - 2034	3.95%	VARIABLE	£1,170.50	£162,648.50	£79,977.01	£82,671.73	£143,327.27
144	May - 2034	3.95%	VARIABLE	£1,170.50	£163,819.00	£80,448.80	£83,370.45	£142,628.55
145	Jun - 2034	3.95%	VARIABLE	£1,170.50	£164,989.50	£80,918.28	£84,071.47	£141,927.53
146	Jul - 2034	3.95%	VARIABLE	£1,170.50	£166,160.00	£81,385.48	£84,774.79	£141,224.21
147	Aug - 2034	3.95%	VARIABLE	£1,170.50	£167,330.50	£81,850.33	£85,480.43	£140,518.57
148	Sep - 2034	3.95%	VARIABLE	£1,170.50	£168,501.00	£82,312.87	£86,188.39	£139,810.61
149	Oct - 2034	3.95%	VARIABLE	£1,170.50	£169,671.50	£82,773.08	£86,898.68	£139,100.32
150	Nov - 2034	3.95%	VARIABLE	£1,170.50	£170,842.00	£83,230.95	£87,611.31	£138,387.69
151	Dec - 2034	3.95%	VARIABLE	£1,170.50	£172,012.50	£83,686.47	£88,326.29	£137,672.71
152	Jan - 2035	3.95%	VARIABLE	£1,170.50	£173,183.00	£84,139.65	£89,043.62	£136,955.38
153	Feb - 2035	3.95%	VARIABLE	£1,170.50	£174,353.50	£84,590.46	£89,763.31	£136,235.69
154	Mar - 2035	3.95%	VARIABLE	£1,170.50	£175,524.00	£85,038.90	£90,485.37	£135,513.63
155	Apr - 2035	3.95%	VARIABLE	£1,170.50	£176,694.50	£85,484.97	£91,209.81	£134,789.19
156	May - 2035	3.95%	VARIABLE	£1,170.50	£177,865.00	£85,928.65	£91,936.63	£134,062.37
157	Jun - 2035	3.95%	VARIABLE	£1,170.50	£179,035.50	£86,369.94	£92,665.84	£133,333.16
158	Jul - 2035	3.95%	VARIABLE	£1,170.50	£180,206.00	£86,808.82	£93,397.45	£132,601.55
159	Aug - 2035	3.95%	VARIABLE	£1,170.50	£181,376.50	£87,245.30	£94,131.48	£131,867.52
160	Sep - 2035	3.95%	VARIABLE	£1,170.50	£182,547.00	£87,679.37	£94,867.91	£131,131.09
161	Oct - 2035	3.95%	VARIABLE	£1,170.50	£183,717.50	£88,111.01	£95,606.78	£130,392.22
162	Nov - 2035	3.95%	VARIABLE	£1,170.50	£184,888.00	£88,540.22	£96,348.07	£129,650.93
163	Dec - 2035	3.95%	VARIABLE	£1,170.50	£186,058.50	£88,966.98	£97,091.81	£128,907.19
164	Jan - 2036	3.95%	VARIABLE	£1,170.50	£187,229.00	£89,391.30	£97,837.99	£128,161.01
165	Feb - 2036	3.95%	VARIABLE	£1,170.50	£188,399.50	£89,813.17	£98,586.63	£127,412.37
166	Mar - 2036	3.95%	VARIABLE	£1,170.50	£189,570.00	£90,232.56	£99,337.73	£126,661.27
167	Apr - 2036	3.95%	VARIABLE	£1,170.50	£190,740.50	£90,649.48	£100,091.31	£125,907.69
168	May - 2036	3.95%	VARIABLE	£1,170.50	£191,911.00	£91,063.94	£100,847.36	£125,151.64
169	Jun - 2036	3.95%	VARIABLE	£1,170.50	£193,081.50	£91,475.90	£101,605.91	£124,393.09
170	Jul - 2036	3.95%	VARIABLE	£1,170.50	£194,252.00	£91,885.36	£102,366.95	£123,632.05
171	Aug - 2036	3.95%	VARIABLE	£1,170.50	£195,422.50	£92,292.31	£103,130.49	£122,868.51
172	Sep - 2036	3.95%	VARIABLE	£1,170.50	£196,593.00	£92,696.75	£103,896.55	£122,102.45
173	Oct - 2036	3.95%	VARIABLE	£1,170.50	£197,763.50	£93,098.67	£104,665.14	£121,333.86
174	Nov - 2036	3.95%	VARIABLE	£1,170.50	£198,934.00	£93,498.06	£105,436.25	£120,562.75
175	Dec - 2036	3.95%	VARIABLE	£1,170.50	£200,104.50	£93,894.92	£106,209.90	£119,789.10
176	Jan - 2037	3.95%	VARIABLE	£1,170.50	£201,275.00	£94,289.22	£106,986.09	£119,012.91
177	Feb - 2037	3.95%	VARIABLE	£1,170.50	£202,445.50	£94,680.97	£107,764.84	£118,234.16
178	Mar - 2037	3.95%	VARIABLE	£1,170.50	£203,616.00	£95,070.16	£108,546.16	£117,452.84
179	Apr - 2037	3.95%	VARIABLE	£1,170.50	£204,786.50	£95,456.78	£109,330.05	£116,668.95
180	May - 2037	3.95%	VARIABLE	£1,170.50	£205,957.00	£95,840.81	£110,116.51	£115,882.49
181	Jun - 2037	3.95%	VARIABLE	£1,170.50	£207,127.50	£96,222.26	£110,905.57	£115,093.43
182	Jul - 2037	3.95%	VARIABLE	£1,170.50	£208,298.00	£96,601.11	£111,697.22	£114,301.78
183	Aug - 2037	3.95%	VARIABLE	£1,170.50	£209,468.50	£96,977.35	£112,491.48	£113,507.52
184	Sep - 2037	3.95%	VARIABLE	£1,170.50	£210,639.00	£97,350.98	£113,288.35	£112,710.65
185	Oct - 2037	3.95%	VARIABLE	£1,170.50	£211,809.50	£97,721.99	£114,087.85	£111,911.15
186	Nov - 2037	3.95%	VARIABLE	£1,170.50	£212,980.00	£98,090.38	£114,889.98	£111,109.02
187	Dec - 2037	3.95%	VARIABLE	£1,170.50	£214,150.50	£98,456.09	£115,694.75	£110,304.25
188	Jan - 2038	3.95%	VARIABLE	£1,170.50	£215,321.00	£98,819.18	£116,502.16	£109,496.84
189	Feb - 2038	3.95%	VARIABLE	£1,170.50	£216,491.50	£99,179.61	£117,312.24	£108,686.76
190	Mar - 2038	3.95%	VARIABLE	£1,170.50	£217,662.00	£99,537.37	£118,124.98	£107,874.02
191	Apr - 2038	3.95%	VARIABLE	£1,170.50	£218,832.50	£99,892.45	£118,940.40	£107,058.60
192	May - 2038	3.95%	VARIABLE	£1,170.50	£220,003.00	£100,244.85	£119,758.50	£106,240.50
193	Jun - 2038	3.95%	VARIABLE	£1,170.50	£221,173.50	£100,594.56	£120,579.29	£105,419.71
194	Jul - 2038	3.95%	VARIABLE	£1,170.50	£222,344.00	£100,941.57	£121,402.79	£104,596.21
195	Aug - 2038	3.95%	VARIABLE	£1,170.50	£223,514.50	£101,285.88	£122,228.99	£103,770.01

196	Sep - 2038	3.95%	VARIABLE	£1,170.50	£224,685.00	£101,627.44	£123,057.82	£102,941.08
197	Oct - 2038	3.95%	VARIABLE	£1,170.50	£225,855.50	£101,966.29	£123,889.57	£102,109.43
198	Nov - 2038	3.95%	VARIABLE	£1,170.50	£227,026.00	£102,302.40	£124,723.98	£101,275.04
199	Dec - 2038	3.95%	VARIABLE	£1,170.50	£228,196.50	£102,635.78	£125,561.10	£100,437.90
200	Jan - 2039	3.95%	VARIABLE	£1,170.50	£229,367.00	£102,966.37	£126,401.00	£99,598.00
201	Feb - 2039	3.95%	VARIABLE	£1,170.50	£230,537.50	£103,294.21	£127,243.66	£98,755.34
202	Mar - 2039	3.95%	VARIABLE	£1,170.50	£231,708.00	£103,619.28	£128,089.09	£97,909.91
203	Apr - 2039	3.95%	VARIABLE	£1,170.50	£232,878.50	£103,941.57	£128,937.30	£97,061.70
204	May - 2039	3.95%	VARIABLE	£1,170.50	£234,049.00	£104,261.06	£129,788.31	£96,210.69
205	Jun - 2039	3.95%	VARIABLE	£1,170.50	£235,219.50	£104,577.76	£130,642.12	£95,356.88
206	Jul - 2039	3.95%	VARIABLE	£1,170.50	£236,390.00	£104,891.64	£131,498.74	£94,500.26
207	Aug - 2039	3.95%	VARIABLE	£1,170.50	£237,560.50	£105,202.70	£132,358.18	£93,640.82
208	Sep - 2039	3.95%	VARIABLE	£1,170.50	£238,731.00	£105,510.94	£133,220.44	£92,778.56
209	Oct - 2039	3.95%	VARIABLE	£1,170.50	£239,901.50	£105,816.33	£134,085.55	£91,913.45
210	Nov - 2039	3.95%	VARIABLE	£1,170.50	£241,072.00	£106,118.88	£134,953.50	£91,045.50
211	Dec - 2039	3.95%	VARIABLE	£1,170.50	£242,242.50	£106,418.57	£135,824.32	£90,174.68
212	Jan - 2040	3.95%	VARIABLE	£1,170.50	£243,413.00	£106,715.40	£136,697.98	£89,301.01
213	Feb - 2040	3.95%	VARIABLE	£1,170.50	£244,583.50	£107,009.35	£137,574.55	£88,424.45
214	Mar - 2040	3.95%	VARIABLE	£1,170.50	£245,754.00	£107,300.41	£138,453.98	£87,545.02
215	Apr - 2040	3.95%	VARIABLE	£1,170.50	£246,924.50	£107,588.56	£139,336.32	£86,662.68
216	May - 2040	3.95%	VARIABLE	£1,170.50	£248,095.00	£107,873.85	£140,221.55	£85,777.45
217	Jun - 2040	3.95%	VARIABLE	£1,170.50	£249,265.50	£108,156.20	£141,109.71	£84,889.29
218	Jul - 2040	3.95%	VARIABLE	£1,170.50	£250,436.00	£108,435.62	£142,000.78	£83,998.22
219	Aug - 2040	3.95%	VARIABLE	£1,170.50	£251,606.50	£108,712.12	£142,894.79	£83,104.21
220	Sep - 2040	3.95%	VARIABLE	£1,170.50	£252,777.00	£108,985.67	£143,791.74	£82,207.26
221	Oct - 2040	3.95%	VARIABLE	£1,170.50	£253,947.50	£109,256.27	£144,691.64	£81,307.36
222	Nov - 2040	3.95%	VARIABLE	£1,170.50	£255,118.00	£109,523.91	£145,594.51	£80,404.49
223	Dec - 2040	3.95%	VARIABLE	£1,170.50	£256,288.50	£109,788.57	£146,500.34	£79,498.66
224	Jan - 2041	3.95%	VARIABLE	£1,170.50	£257,459.00	£110,050.25	£147,409.16	£78,589.84
225	Feb - 2041	3.95%	VARIABLE	£1,170.50	£258,629.50	£110,308.94	£148,320.97	£77,678.03
226	Mar - 2041	3.95%	VARIABLE	£1,170.50	£259,800.00	£110,564.63	£149,235.79	£76,763.21
227	Apr - 2041	3.95%	VARIABLE	£1,170.50	£260,970.50	£110,817.31	£150,153.61	£75,845.39
228	May - 2041	3.95%	VARIABLE	£1,170.50	£262,141.00	£111,066.97	£151,074.45	£74,924.55
229	Jun - 2041	3.95%	VARIABLE	£1,170.50	£263,311.50	£111,313.60	£151,998.33	£74,000.67
230	Jul - 2041	3.95%	VARIABLE	£1,170.50	£264,482.00	£111,557.18	£152,925.25	£73,073.75
231	Aug - 2041	3.95%	VARIABLE	£1,170.50	£265,652.50	£111,797.72	£153,855.21	£72,143.79
232	Sep - 2041	3.95%	VARIABLE	£1,170.50	£266,823.00	£112,035.19	£154,788.24	£71,210.76
233	Oct - 2041	3.95%	VARIABLE	£1,170.50	£267,993.50	£112,269.59	£155,724.34	£70,274.66
234	Nov - 2041	3.95%	VARIABLE	£1,170.50	£269,164.00	£112,500.91	£156,663.52	£69,335.48
235	Dec - 2041	3.95%	VARIABLE	£1,170.50	£270,334.50	£112,729.14	£157,605.80	£68,393.20
236	Jan - 2042	3.95%	VARIABLE	£1,170.50	£271,505.00	£112,954.27	£158,551.17	£67,447.83
237	Feb - 2042	3.95%	VARIABLE	£1,170.50	£272,675.50	£113,176.29	£159,499.66	£66,499.34
238	Mar - 2042	3.95%	VARIABLE	£1,170.50	£273,846.00	£113,395.18	£160,451.27	£65,547.73
239	Apr - 2042	3.95%	VARIABLE	£1,170.50	£275,016.50	£113,610.94	£161,406.01	£64,592.99
240	May - 2042	3.95%	VARIABLE	£1,170.50	£276,187.00	£113,823.56	£162,363.89	£63,635.11
241	Jun - 2042	3.95%	VARIABLE	£1,170.50	£277,357.50	£114,033.03	£163,324.93	£62,674.07
242	Jul - 2042	3.95%	VARIABLE	£1,170.50	£278,528.00	£114,239.33	£164,289.13	£61,709.87
243	Aug - 2042	3.95%	VARIABLE	£1,170.50	£279,698.50	£114,442.46	£165,256.50	£60,742.50
244	Sep - 2042	3.95%	VARIABLE	£1,170.50	£280,869.00	£114,642.40	£166,227.06	£59,771.94
245	Oct - 2042	3.95%	VARIABLE	£1,170.50	£282,039.50	£114,839.15	£167,200.81	£58,798.19
246	Nov - 2042	3.95%	VARIABLE	£1,170.50	£283,210.00	£115,032.69	£168,177.77	£57,821.23
247	Dec - 2042	3.95%	VARIABLE	£1,170.50	£284,380.50	£115,223.02	£169,157.94	£56,841.06
248	Jan - 2043	3.95%	VARIABLE	£1,170.50	£285,551.00	£115,410.12	£170,141.34	£55,857.66
249	Feb - 2043	3.95%	VARIABLE	£1,170.50	£286,721.50	£115,593.99	£171,127.98	£54,871.02
250	Mar - 2043	3.95%	VARIABLE	£1,170.50	£287,892.00	£115,774.61	£172,117.87	£53,881.13
251	Apr - 2043	3.95%	VARIABLE	£1,170.50	£289,062.50	£115,951.96	£173,111.01	£52,887.99
252	May - 2043	3.95%	VARIABLE	£1,170.50	£290,233.00	£116,126.05	£174,107.42	£51,891.58
253	Jun - 2043	3.95%	VARIABLE	£1,170.50	£291,403.50	£116,296.86	£175,107.11	£50,891.89
254	Jul - 2043	3.95%	VARIABLE	£1,170.50	£292,574.00	£116,464.38	£176,110.10	£49,888.90
255	Aug - 2043	3.95%	VARIABLE	£1,170.50	£293,744.50	£116,628.60	£177,116.38	£48,882.62
256	Sep - 2043	3.95%	VARIABLE	£1,170.50	£294,915.00	£116,789.51	£178,125.98	£47,873.02
257	Oct - 2043	3.95%	VARIABLE	£1,170.50	£296,085.50	£116,947.09	£179,138.90	£46,860.10
258	Nov - 2043	3.95%	VARIABLE	£1,170.50	£297,256.00	£117,101.34	£180,155.15	£45,843.85
259	Dec - 2043	3.95%	VARIABLE	£1,170.50	£298,426.50	£117,252.24	£181,174.75	£44,824.25
260	Jan - 2044	3.95%	VARIABLE	£1,170.50	£299,597.00	£117,399.79	£182,197.71	£43,801.29
261	Feb - 2044	3.95%	VARIABLE	£1,170.50	£300,767.50	£117,543.98	£183,224.03	£42,774.97
262	Mar - 2044	3.95%	VARIABLE	£1,170.50	£301,938.00	£117,684.77	£184,253.73	£41,745.27

263	Apr - 2044	3.95%	VARIABLE	£1,170.50	£303,108.50	£117,822.18	£185,286.82	£40,712.18
264	May - 2044	3.95%	VARIABLE	£1,170.50	£304,279.00	£117,956.19	£186,323.31	£39,675.69
265	Jun - 2044	3.95%	VARIABLE	£1,170.50	£305,449.50	£118,086.79	£187,363.22	£38,635.78
266	Jul - 2044	3.95%	VARIABLE	£1,170.50	£306,620.00	£118,213.96	£188,406.54	£37,592.46
267	Aug - 2044	3.95%	VARIABLE	£1,170.50	£307,790.50	£118,337.70	£189,453.30	£36,545.70
268	Sep - 2044	3.95%	VARIABLE	£1,170.50	£308,961.00	£118,458.00	£190,503.51	£35,495.49
269	Oct - 2044	3.95%	VARIABLE	£1,170.50	£310,131.50	£118,574.84	£191,557.17	£34,441.83
270	Nov - 2044	3.95%	VARIABLE	£1,170.50	£311,302.00	£118,688.21	£192,614.30	£33,384.70
271	Dec - 2044	3.95%	VARIABLE	£1,170.50	£312,472.50	£118,798.10	£193,674.91	£32,324.09
272	Jan - 2045	3.95%	VARIABLE	£1,170.50	£313,643.00	£118,904.50	£194,739.02	£31,259.98
273	Feb - 2045	3.95%	VARIABLE	£1,170.50	£314,813.50	£119,007.40	£195,806.62	£30,192.38
274	Mar - 2045	3.95%	VARIABLE	£1,170.50	£315,984.00	£119,106.76	£196,877.74	£29,121.26
275	Apr - 2045	3.95%	VARIABLE	£1,170.50	£317,154.50	£119,202.64	£197,952.38	£28,046.62
276	May - 2045	3.95%	VARIABLE	£1,170.50	£318,325.00	£119,294.96	£199,030.57	£26,968.43
277	Jun - 2045	3.95%	VARIABLE	£1,170.50	£319,495.50	£119,383.73	£200,112.30	£25,886.70
278	Jul - 2045	3.95%	VARIABLE	£1,170.50	£320,666.00	£119,468.94	£201,197.59	£24,801.41
279	Aug - 2045	3.95%	VARIABLE	£1,170.50	£321,836.50	£119,550.56	£202,286.45	£23,712.55
280	Sep - 2045	3.95%	VARIABLE	£1,170.50	£323,007.00	£119,628.63	£203,378.90	£22,620.10
281	Oct - 2045	3.95%	VARIABLE	£1,170.50	£324,177.50	£119,703.09	£204,474.94	£21,524.06
282	Nov - 2045	3.95%	VARIABLE	£1,170.50	£325,348.00	£119,773.94	£205,574.60	£20,424.40
283	Dec - 2045	3.95%	VARIABLE	£1,170.50	£326,518.50	£119,841.17	£206,677.87	£19,321.13
284	Jan - 2046	3.95%	VARIABLE	£1,170.50	£327,689.00	£119,904.77	£207,784.77	£18,214.23
285	Feb - 2046	3.95%	VARIABLE	£1,170.50	£328,859.50	£119,964.73	£208,895.32	£17,103.68
286	Mar - 2046	3.95%	VARIABLE	£1,170.50	£330,030.00	£120,021.03	£210,009.52	£15,989.48
287	Apr - 2046	3.95%	VARIABLE	£1,170.50	£331,200.50	£120,073.66	£211,127.39	£14,871.61
288	May - 2046	3.95%	VARIABLE	£1,170.50	£332,371.00	£120,122.61	£212,248.94	£13,750.06
289	Jun - 2046	3.95%	VARIABLE	£1,170.50	£333,541.50	£120,167.87	£213,374.18	£12,624.82
290	Jul - 2046	3.95%	VARIABLE	£1,170.50	£334,712.00	£120,209.43	£214,503.13	£11,495.87
291	Aug - 2046	3.95%	VARIABLE	£1,170.50	£335,882.50	£120,247.27	£215,635.79	£10,363.21
292	Sep - 2046	3.95%	VARIABLE	£1,170.50	£337,053.00	£120,281.38	£216,772.18	£9,226.82
293	Oct - 2046	3.95%	VARIABLE	£1,170.50	£338,223.50	£120,311.75	£217,912.31	£8,086.69
294	Nov - 2046	3.95%	VARIABLE	£1,170.50	£339,394.00	£120,338.37	£219,056.19	£6,942.81
295	Dec - 2046	3.95%	VARIABLE	£1,170.50	£340,564.50	£120,361.22	£220,203.84	£5,795.16
296	Jan - 2047	3.95%	VARIABLE	£1,170.50	£341,735.00	£120,380.30	£221,355.27	£4,643.73
297	Feb - 2047	3.95%	VARIABLE	£1,170.50	£342,905.50	£120,395.59	£222,510.46	£3,488.52
298	Mar - 2047	3.95%	VARIABLE	£1,170.50	£344,076.00	£120,407.07	£223,669.50	£2,329.50
299	Apr - 2047	3.95%	VARIABLE	£1,170.50	£345,246.50	£120,414.74	£224,832.34	£1,166.66
300	May - 2047	3.95%	VARIABLE	£1,170.50	£346,417.00	£120,418.56	£225,999.00	£0.00

REFERENCES

1. **Risk Spectrum diagram - Courtesy**
www.bing.com/images

2. **National Insurance**
https://www.gov.uk/national-insurance/print

3. **State Pension**
https://www.gov.uk/new-state-pension/print

https://www.gov.uk/topic/business-tax/pension-scheme-administration

4. **Pension Simplifications**
Pensions tax simplification 2006 (thepfs.org)

5. **Vanguard Investor**
Introducing Vanguard Personal Financial Planning | Vanguard UK Investor (vanguardinvestor.co.uk)

6. **Investor Behavior – DALBAR**
2019-dalbar.pdf (cswadvisors.org)

Printed in Great Britain
by Amazon